READ YOUR BIBLE FOR ALL IT'S WORTH

YOUR

BIBLE

FOR

ALL IT'S WORTH

*Finally! Easy Help to Understand
the Greatest Book Ever Written!*

ANDY TAYLOR

FOREWORD BY JACK R. TAYLOR

Lizzy

Blessings.

Is 40:8

WHAT OTHERS ARE SAYING ABOUT
READING YOUR BIBLE FOR ALL IT'S WORTH

"What an imaginative title and what a lofty suggestion: *READING YOUR BIBLE FOR ALL IT'S WORTH*. If you have granted the Bible the credibility to open it and read from its contents, this helpful treatise could make you a world-class lover of the Bible and a powerful champion of its life-changing truths."

Bill Johnson
Bethel Church, Redding, CA

"I read once that a genius is one who has the ability to make complicated concepts simple. If that is true, Andy Taylor is a genius! This little book makes the "Big Book" much less intimidating. Thank you, Andy, for helping us all read the Bible for all its worth! Five stars from me."

Clark Whitten,
Founding Pastor, Grace Church, Orlando , FL

"Anyone can read the Bible. It's how you "read the Bible" that determines whether or not the Bible can lead you. Andy Taylor, in *Reading Your Bible For All It's Worth*, has been able to assist those who want to get the most out of their time in God's Word. For thousands of years, believers have been in conversations on how to approach, get the most out of, and how to understand the heart of God in scripture. Here is your chance to jump into this conversation and start *Reading Your Bible For All It's Worth*."

Ty Bean
Pastor, Cowboy Junction Church, Hobbs, NM

Andy Taylor stands tall in the midst of the best of them. His calling card is love; his signature is compassion for all people. Reminiscent of fellow Oklahoman and cowboy wit Will Rogers, Andy inspires and stirs us through the truth, insights, and humor of his stories. Captured in the same simplicity as in the days they were written, his stories beckon us to travel on a similar journey as men and women of old. Andy began his journey by discovering the love of God and invites us to join him and experience that life-altering awe and love. Grab this opportunity to find your truth in the book Andy reveals as Truth. Enjoy!

David VanCronkhite,
Agape Transformation, Atlanta, GA

www.BurkhartBooks.com
Bedford, Texas

DEDICATION

This book is dedicated to Ronnie Chadwick. Ronnie was my first, and really the only Pastor I've ever had. I came to the Lord at 30 years of age, and not growing up in church, I had a hundred dumb questions about God, the Bible and anything else spiritual. The only thing I had going for me was that I did believe in God and, somehow, I knew without a doubt that He was good. Ronnie, or "Preacher," as I fondly call him helped me with the answers to all those dumb questions without ever making me feel dumb. I remember, more times than I can recall, sitting at his and Ruth's (his wife) kitchen table when I'd ask one of those questions. His response was nearly always the same. In his deep baritone voice, He'd say, "Well, Andy, what does the Word say?" We would open our Bibles, he would guide me along, and we'd dig until we found an adequate answer. I had no idea at the time how this would imprint me in such a profound way in my own study of the Word or how it would affect me in such a deep, positive way for the rest of my life. It has been invaluable!

Ronnie had a love for the Word of God, something I see as a rarity these days. His love for the written Word was contagious. I caught it long before I felt called into the ministry. I'm deeply grateful for that.

Ronnie has pastored for over 40 years and is now in an assisted living center in Edmond, Oklahoma, still teaching the Word and imparting the love for it. I can only pray that I can be half as effective and faithful as he has been!

ACKNOWLEDGMENTS

The Family at Trinity Fellowship
Sayre, Oklahoma

What a totally unique bunch of people this is! Extraordinary, to put it mildly. Their love and support for me through the good and the bad is nothing short of miraculous. They have been patient with me when I knew very little and was as green as a gourd, and we have grown up in the Word together. What a Family! Thanks from the bottom of my heart!

The Guys Around the Office

Daryle, Buddy, Cody, Eric, Kenny, Charlie, Mike and a dozen or more others who roam in and out on a totally unscheduled basis, but the discussions we have about the kingdom of God and everything attached to it have helped us all get a better grip on the Word than any of us would've ever had otherwise. Those times have been, not only an incredible blessing but a great learning experience for me, as well. I treasure your wisdom, but not nearly as much as I treasure your friendship!

I've known David Clark only a few years but in that short time he's had a profound impact on my life. A seasoned veteran of national as well as international ministry, founding ministry schools in Mexico and South America and author of nine books. His knowledge of the historical details of the Bible has helped me to be a much better teacher than I would have been otherwise. He believes deeply in what we're doing here and is a very important part of the "team"at Trinity Fellowship. This book wouldn't have happened without him urging me to do it. Thank you, David!

A Few "Big Brothers"

David VanCronkhite, Tim Johns, John Wallace, David Kula, and Ben Fike. You guys have blessed me more than you could possibly imagine. Your wisdom, encouragement, prophetic insight and friendship have made my life richer than it would've ever been otherwise. Thanks for believing in me and always lifting me to a higher place!

Uncle Jack

Jack Taylor, you've been the perfect example for the Taylor family. From my earliest remembrance of riding with you at about age five to preach in the big metropolis of Gageby, Texas, (population about ten), to the quality time we have these days, you have been pouring into me and nurturing my walk with the Father. Even those years none of us were in church and didn't want to be, you were always there for us. Your wisdom and guidance have been unwavering. Your encouragement to me in my role as a leader has sustained me at some very critical times. Thank you for always pushing me to go farther! You're just my Uncle in the natural, but a Father in the Spirit! I love you, and I'm forever grateful to you.

My Own Family

Mom & Dad

Cliff and Charlene Taylor, still the most remarkable people I've ever known. To have parents like I've had and not attempt to do something noteworthy with your life would be a catastrophic miss. They taught us all the right things, but the things that stand out above everything else is that, even though we didn't go to church, they imparted to us the reality that God is real, and that God is good! I can't imagine how my life would have gone not knowing that! Good job!

My Brother

Monty Taylor, my best friend and partner in crime since the day you were born. Thanks for always being there, for always having my back and for being one of the most solid people I've ever known.

My Kids and Grandkids

Clint, Kristy, Cooper, Dailee, Preslie, and Crockett; Cade and Allie; Cole, Kelly, Calli, Maverick, and Knox; Clay, Chelsea, Timber, and Asa Cliff (arriving in March '19!); Cord, who left early for Heaven and beautiful Cameron, the icing on the cake after five boys!

Julie

I can't say enough! From age 13 you have been my soulmate through life. It was literally a 'match made in heaven'! Through all the mountains and valleys of life, we're still standing, and life gets sweeter by the day! You're so much more than I could've ever hoped or asked for! Still the most beautiful person I've ever known, inside and out! I love you!

The Taylors are some pretty incredible, and unique people. You all have given me the grit and determination to keep going when quitting would have been the easiest thing. You are the motivation for me not to give up, to make my life count and to do it in a noble way. You make me want to leave behind, a legacy of not just being a "hearer," but to be a doer of the Word, someone who trusted God at His Word, and swung for the fence with his life. My life would be dismal and boring without y'all. Because of you, I'm rich! I owe everything to you!

CONTENTS

FOREWORD

DO NOT PROCEED BEFORE READING THIS!

I am gripped by the words in the title of this treatise, "... for all its worth." My response to this striking statement is: No one in history, absolutely no one, has read the Bible for all it's worth. There has never been a book, and there will never be one, that is loaded with such benefits as the Bible. I suggest an exercise for everyone who chooses to read this small but significant book:

Pick up a Bible; the one closest will do. You are holding in your hand the greatest collection of Truth ever to be presented to mankind. In fact, it is the combined result of multiplied miracles. Yes, I said it: the BIBLE IS A MIRACLE! Up to now you have read the Bible, memorized its verses, appreciated its riches and applied its principles according to your evaluation of it. Read the following slowly and carefully. It would likely help to read it several times. It's about the Bible itself.

With the exception of Jesus Himself, the Bible is Heaven's greatest single gift to Planet Earth. Hands down! From its pages, we are informed of our sin, man's lostness, God's offered remedy and our intended eternal destiny! Its internal testimony is that it is "God-breathed," that is, its pages are literally the distillation of the breath of God. Thus, when you read its contents, the same Spirit that first breathed it breathes on it again and offers, not just information, but revelation. In that sense "life" awaits your reading the Bible!

Allow me to sum it up:

This Bible is miraculous in it ORIGINATION! This is summed up in the miracle of INSPIRATION which is that work of the Spirit of God on the human authors that made their writings a record of divine revelation.

This Bible is miraculous in its CONTINUATION! This is summed up in the miracle of PRESERVATION, that work of the Spirit of God on the processes of Scripture and those who translated its contents which guarantees the arrival of God's intended information in every successive generation with its message intact.

This Bible is miraculous in its REVELATION! This is summed up in the miracle of ILLUMINATION, that work of the Spirit of God on the mind and life of the reader which offers to the simplest mind a level of learning that transcends the realms of natural understanding.

You might be thinking, "This information is heavy, and I don't understand it!" That's just it! You have a common component in each of these above described miracles, namely "that work of the Spirit of God!"

Think of it like this: The moment you picked up your Bible the same Spirit who created the world, raised Jesus from the dead, has worked through the ages to redeem what the enemy has stolen, and now lives in you, is ready to guide you in truth—all truth! Allow Him to continue His work through your Bible.

This simple treatise by Andy Taylor, my biological nephew, and my spiritual son will surprise you and leave you with a desire to find in the Bible, the Book of all books just what you needed. This book, *Reading Your Bible for All It's Worth*, is very likely to acquaint you with a life resulting in finding in Jesus all He is worth, working in you to find out all you are worth. To be perfectly frank with you, my bottom-line response to this work left me with a sense of wanting to grab the nearest Bible and begin to read it like I had never read it before, this time "for all it's worth!"

Now, keep your Bible close and read this book with the expectation to find "All it's worth!"

Thanks, Andy, for this simple and yet profound work. Now finish that book on the Father. The World is Waiting!

Jack Taylor,
President, Dimensions Ministries,
Melbourne Florida

INTRODUCTION

The Bible is the most read, referred to, revered, trusted, respected book that mankind has ever been exposed to. After all, it IS the Word of God. It even says of itself, "All scripture is given by inspiration of God."

But, what I've learned in 30 years of shepherding the people of God is that there's not much out there to help the common man learn to read, and become a serious student of the Bible. It seems obvious to me that if we had some simple, easy to understand and solid principles for reading the Bible that millions more would be likely to pick it up more often and glean from the profound wisdom (which is only one of hundreds of benefits) that resides in it. Think of the ramifications of that!

Who's this book for: Well, in a word, "everyone!"

I'm a reader! I love to read. I thank Edith Yowell and Nellie Millar for that. Those two incredible people were my first and second-grade teachers and, along with helping to teach me to read, (my Mom and Dad had me well along the way before I started to school), they imparted to me the joy of reading. I'm profoundly indebted to them for that gift!

I've observed over the years that most people are "nonreaders," especially men. I think it's a tragic phenomenon. What if books were written in such a way to cater to those "nonreaders?" Shorter chapters, more concise content, nutrient-dense, to borrow a phrase. That's how this book is written. For the millions out there who don't like to read but would like to pick up their Bible and be able to read it—more importantly, understand what they are reading—this book is for you!

If you're one of the many people who say, "I try to read my Bible, but I don't understand it." Well, don't lose heart, this book is for you! The principles contained herein, in bite size form, and if ascribed to will enable you to read your Bible with new excitement, knowing you're drawing from the most important Book ever written. These principles will guide your life, give you a Biblical worldview, and acquaint you with the indescribable love of the Father!

Enjoy!

The Anvil of God's Word

Last eve I paused beside the blacksmith's door,
And heard the anvil ring the vesper chime;
Then looking in, I saw upon the floor,
Old hammers, worn with beating years of time.
"How many anvils have you had," said I,
"To wear and batter all these hammers so?
Just one," said he, and then with twinkling eye,
"The anvil wears the hammers out, you know."
And so, I thought, the Anvil of God's Word
For ages skeptic blows have beat upon;
Yet, though the noise of falling blows was heard,
The Anvil is unharmed, the hammers gone.

John Clifford

READ THIS FIRST!

I see this phrase often these days, mostly when I buy and open a new product. If what I've purchased requires some assembly or startup instructions, it's important that I read the instructions, to begin with, before I proceed. By doing so, I can avoid potential problems that might occur. Those little, "Read This First," pages are always very brief but contain vital information in the successful use of the product.

So, whatever you do: READ THIS FIRST! It will help you get started with the right mindset. And, when you begin your journey with the Bible, you will avoid many of the pitfalls that have confused thousands along the way.

God is Good!
God is a Father!
The Father Loves You!
The Father has given You a Kingdom!
The Father wants you to succeed!
The Father wants you to know His Word!
The Father wants you to understand His Word, and His Spirit   will help you!
The Father wants you to read and understand His Word through the lens of grace!
The Father wants the "written" Word to lead you to an encounter with Him!
The Father wants you to "know" Him!
The Father wants you and Him to experience Life together!

It's simple, don't complicate it! These fundamental things will get you headed out in the right direction. I would suggest that when you happen onto a problem verse, or chapter, (which will inevitably happen) that you quickly turn back to this page and read through this short list again, to remind you what's important. It'll help you to regain the right focus as you proceed.

Disclaimer: There have been a few times that I went forward with my product without reading the "Read This First" thing, only to have to return and get it right from the start!

SECTION 1

MY STORY

HOW I CAME TO LOVE THE BIBLE

My marriage to my childhood sweetheart Julie, the love of my life, was in turmoil and deteriorating, my fault. Soon we separated. Now, there was no way our marriage was ever going to work. Within a long five months, I became as discouraged and depressed as a man could possibly get. I saw myself losing everything that was important to me. On that night—I will never, ever forget November 17, 1984—with everything wrong in my life that could be wrong, I sat on the edge of my bed, tears were running down my face, and as I cried uncontrollably, I began to pray the most profound prayer I'd ever prayed, even to this day. Nope, it wasn't very professional sounding because I hadn't had much practice. But it was profound, nonetheless!

"God, if you're out there, you gotta help me!"

And because I'm writing this, you know He did!

It didn't happen overnight, but it started immediately. You've got to know I knew nothing about trusting God; I knew nothing about walking by faith; I didn't even know a relationship with God was anything you could or should do. I was just in a place of painful desperation. Even with a great family and a lot of good friends I was in a place where no one could help me but God.

Now, I was developing a relationship with the Father. I didn't have that terminology then, it would come sometime later. But I soon began to realize and understand more and more about a relationship with my God, who I now know wants us to relate to Him as Father. And, what I thought was the worst time in my life turned out to be the best.

Julie and I were soon back together.

We can all look at our lives and see the many ways God has blessed us, but for me, I'd have to say the two ways He has blessed me the most are: 1) I met the Father before I was exposed to religion and even the church. 2) God has given me an ability to make this thing of relationship with Him as Father as simple as it's really supposed to be!

His Spirit was the One Who gave me that hunger for the Word. All I did was yield to it. I can easily say that today, 35 years later, I'm still hungry for His Word and I love it more today than ever. That's how I came to love the Bible.

Yield to His Spirit, and you'll have that hunger too!

IT'S ALWAYS ABOUT THE ENCOUNTER!

"You can learn a lot about God by reading the Bible, but you can only know Him by giving Him access to your life."

—Andy Taylor

Occasionally I'll make a FaceBook post to cause people to stop and think, or maybe post something that, at face value, challenges traditional religious thinking. I did so a while back with this particular post, "If your Bible reading doesn't eventually lead you into an encounter with the Father, you might be wasting your time.". Boy, did that draw some 'unfriendly' fire!! I was accused of being a heretic by at least one person, false teacher by a couple more….and one guy who stated that he knew me and said that I didn't have due respect for the Bible, anyway, …..and that this was typical thinking for me. All those things are far from the truth, but it reveals how normal Christian thinking goes in the Bible Belt. You see, Bible reading holds such a sacred place in the hearts of believers that anything, or anyone in this instance, that would ever dare to challenge that would be considered false or downright blasphemous.

There were even people in our own camp who seemed to 'turn on me' a little. It made me wonder if I should have made the post at all. But, after reading all the negative feedback and then re-reading my original post, I landed far on the side of, "I still agree with the content that I posted." If you can think about it from an 'unbiased' position, I think you'll begin to agree.

One friend posted, "Well, since we don't know when that encounter is going to happen, we need to keep reading until it does." I don't disagree at all. But, what if we knew 'going in' that's what the Book is designed for in the first place? Then the encounter would be a guarantee. It would be a guarantee since that's what we go looking for in the first place. When we look for the Lord, I mean sincerely look for Him, we will always find Him!

Another friend wrote, "We will never know the God of the Word until we know the Word of God.". I honestly believe that in his mind he thought he was agreeing with me. I do, however, have a problem with that line of thinking. I wanted to (but chose not to further the argument) reply, "So, you're saying we need to be able to read to know God?". That is a real problem in that in Bible times a huge chunk of the general population were illiterate. You can find out a lot of things about God by reading the Bible. I suggest you do so. But, you can only 'know' Him by giving Him access to your life!

Being able to read is not a prerequisite to knowing God!

Nobody we read about in the Bible knew God from what was written. It only happened as a result of personal interaction! It's all about the encounter!!

Those who argue against this line of logic erroneously believe they are protecting and defending the integrity of the Scriptures. But what they're actually doing is fighting against the chief purpose of the written Word in the first place!

A ministry friend of mine went on an elk hunting trip in a remote area of mountainous Colorado. His intention was not to hunt elk but to just get out in the wide-open spaces and spend some 'alone' time with the Lord. He was out on a high rocky ledge overlooking thousands of acres of beautiful and majestic mountains and valleys in the Rocky Mountains. As he was telling me this story, he said, "I was out there by myself; it was just the Lord and me." When he said those words that still small voice of the Lord spoke silently to my heart, "It's always just you and Me!" As he continued his story he said, "Lord, give me a message." He said he immediately heard that same still small voice say to him, "Don't come to Me looking for a message; come looking for Me, and I'll give you a message!" I don't know about you, but it sounds to me exactly like something the Lord might say!

It's imperative that we understand one extremely important thing anytime we open our Bible. I sincerely believe that from God's perspective He has always intended for your entire existence to be about the encounter. What encounter, you might innocently ask? Well, it's the encounter of all encounters; the encounter with Him! Jesus put it in as clear terms as could possibly be stated, "You search the Scriptures, for in them you think you have eternal life; and these are they which testify of Me. But you are not willing to come to Me that you may have life." It was both a chastisement and an invitation at the same time. The stiff-necked, hard-hearted Jews and Pharisees, who prided themselves in their knowledge and interpretation of the Holy Scriptures, made it all about what was "written." I do not disregard that what was written in those days was of utmost importance (as it also is today!) in terms of universal Truth. But, what the religious community in that era failed to awaken to was the reality "that which was written" was written, first and foremost, to help them to meet and then to engage, in a one-on-one relationship with the Creator of the Universe! It's happening on an even grander scale in our generation today! There's not a greater invitation to be given or received that comes anywhere close, in life or in eternity, to this invitation! We don't need to miss it!

When you open your Bible don't go looking for knowledge; go looking for HIM. You'll find Him (that's a guarantee!) and the icing on the cake is that you'll find tons of knowledge, too!

Are you looking for knowledge, or are you looking for Him?

When you start to see your Bible this way it will revolutionize your reading/study and what's even more important it'll enhance your relationship with the Father!

If you miss this part, you've missed the most important part!

As much as I love the written Word of God, my relationship is not with the Book, but with the Father and the Son the Book tells about!

Don't make it difficult. If what I'm saying is true, and I'm betting my life on it, then it should be the easiest thing in the world to connect relationally with the Father! In fact, He wants this relationship I'm talking about even more than you could want it!

So, Interact! Talk to Him! Listen to Him! And, by all means, when you open your Bible plan for an encounter with Him! It's really what it's all about!

ENGAGE:

There's no better time to have an encounter with the Father than now! There's nothing difficult about it. In fact, it might just be the easiest thing you'll ever do. Just try to think about it from God's perspective. You're His hand-picked son/daughter; He loves you as much as He loves Jesus; He wants you to experience His love and presence firsthand!

- Stop what you're doing
- Get your focus off any distractions
- Get your focus on the Lord
- Listen for His still, small voice
- If you don't hear anything, don't worry
- Just relax in His presence
- When you do talk to Him, address Him as Father, Daddy, Papa …or whatever seems natural for you.
- Don't hurry
- Enjoy!
- Make this a habit

We have the written Word to lead us into an encounter with the Father. Make sure you don't lose sight of that!

YOU HAVE A HELPER!

"The Bible applied to the heart by the Holy Spirit is the chief means by which men are built up and established in the faith."
—J.C. Ryle

A sometimes overlooked benefit is the incredible help you can tap into when you begin to read your Bible, from the Holy Spirit. This point will be found scattered through the entire scope of this book to remind you that He's there to help. I don't want to be redundant, but without the Holy Spirit's help, you're going to limit yourself in your understanding of spiritual things. You can, however, read the Bible without His influence and receive lots of good information, if that's what you're looking for. But, any serious student of the Bible would be doing themselves a favor if they would, at the very beginning, lean on the wisdom of the Holy Spirit. Even His name in the Greek language reveals this facet of His character; "Paraklete"—One called alongside to help!

The Holy Spirit searches all things of God, "yes the deep things of God." He knows the beginning from the end. He's the Author and Finisher of your faith. He will show you things to come. He helps you to pray when you don't know what, or how to pray. He's "your comforter." He knows the will of the Father for you at every turn. He's your Teacher! All these and more are benefits of learning to be sensitive to the Holy Spirit in every instance. But, the real icing on the cake is the way He reveals God to you! He presents Him as a loving Father. One Who longs to know you and to be interactive and intimate with you. A Father that never makes a mistake with His kids. One Who is there at all times to nurture and love us through all the ups and downs of life's events.

But as it is written: "Eye has not seen, nor ear heard, Nor have entered into the heart of man the things which God has prepared for those who love Him."

But God has revealed them to us through His Spirit. For the Spirit searches all things, yes, the deep things of God. For what man knows the things of a man except the spirit of the man which is in him? Even so, no one knows the things of God except the Spirit of God. Now we have received, not the spirit of the world, but the Spirit who is from God, that we might know the things that have been freely given to us by God.

These things we also speak, not in words which man's wisdom teaches but which the Holy Spirit teaches, comparing spiritual things with spiritual. But the natural man does not receive the things of the Spirit of God, for they are foolishness to him; nor can he know them, because they are spiritually discerned.

1 Cor 2:9-15

These things I have spoken to you while being present with you. But the Helper, the Holy Spirit, whom the Father will send in My name, He will teach you all things, and bring to your remembrance all things that I said to you.

John 14:25-26

Start now to listen and rely on the wisdom and guidance of the Holy Spirit. When you do that, the Word becomes alive! He's your Helper!

ENGAGE:

When you open your Bible to read, stop and ask the Holy Spirit to rise up in you. Yield yourself over to Him and ask Him to guide your reading. Tell Him that you desire His help in reading and understanding what you read. Start now learning to be sensitive to what He is doing in you and what He's saying to you about what you are reading. Make this a habit, and before long it will become second nature to you.

YOUR BIGGEST CHALLENGE: "CAN YOU CHANGE YOUR MIND?"

"Men do not reject the Bible because it contradicts itself but because it contradicts them."

—Author Unknown

It is truly one of the great challenges of the Christian faith. The Jews in Jesus' day refused to do it. Most of the Scribes and Pharisees didn't even try. And, thousands of believers in our own generation can't do it either. It seems simple but thirty years of observation and experience has proven to me that it's as difficult as anything we are confronted with in our Christian life.

CAN YOU CHANGE YOUR MIND?

Principles run deep. Things you learned as a child, no matter what religious environment you may have grown up in, take root in the soul as truth and almost nothing can alter them. Most, if not all, have an element of truth about them but just like anything else, there are still more levels of truth to be understood if, and only if, one is willing to be taught. As a veteran teacher of the Word, I will say that a teachable spirit is something I put a high value on. I often get criticized for repeating myself. I don't particularly enjoy that criticism, but my goal as a leader is to get everyone on the same page. When you think about that from my perspective, it begins to become clearer. The apostle Paul, possibly dealing with the same "religious" attitudes says in Phil 3:1:

For me to write the same things to you is not tedious, but for you it is safe.

Repetition is good. It helps to plant and establish the Word in people's hearts. It takes repetition for many people to get their breakthrough in learning new information. I was teaching a series some years back in helping people to learn to function in personal prophecy. A woman who grew up in a very traditional conservative church environment told me, "I've been hearing you say that for eight years and I finally got it tonight!" That's not as rare as you might think. In fact, I believe it's probably a prevalent attitude in the Bible Belt, if not everywhere in religious circles.

I find myself often giving the advice, "Don't tie the ends up!" By that I mean, don't close the book on what you think you know. If you tie the ends up, you'll quickly become rigid and unteachable. You'll find yourself intolerant of anyone's viewpoint that might differ from yours. But, the most serious thing that can happen is that you'll close yourself off, even, from the Holy Spirit as He attempts to teach you deeper truths.

Decide right now to be willing and flexible to change your mind on new enlightenment from the Holy Spirit. Learn to listen to the opinions and positions of other people. You might just find yourself growing into a much broader perspective. If you can do this, you'll set yourself apart from most of the world's Christian population.

CAN YOU CHANGE YOUR MIND?

If you can, you'll never stop growing!

THE WORD, THE FATHER, THE SON, THE SPIRIT, AND THEIR KINGDOM

"And this gospel of the kingdom will be preached in all the world as a witness to all the nations, and then the end will come."

—Jesus

You might ask why a chapter on The Father, The Son, The Spirit, and Their kingdom would be included in a book teaching people how to read their Bible. It's simple. If you can't begin to understand the kingdom, you'll never understand the Bible!

When Jesus came onto the scene, everything changed. He came to establish His Father's kingdom, which was vastly different than what the Pharisees had expected. They knew that the Messiah was coming, but they couldn't reconcile in their own minds that this, Jesus, was the One. As far as they were concerned He was just the illegitimate son of a carpenter. It's sad, but the Jewish religious leaders had become so self-righteous that they missed the Son of God living in their very midst. When Jesus began to teach, He said things such as, "You have heard it said, but I say to you". The Pharisees knew what the Word said; they didn't know what it meant! Jesus' faithfulness exposed their faithlessness, and they hated Him for it.

Jesus' kingdom is a kingdom built and established on love; not the ordinary brotherly love that the world had experienced but a much higher and more powerful, and deeper quality of love; agape, that perfect, giving kind of love. The Pharisees put all their emphasis on the outward appearance of things while Jesus' focus was the heart. He even told them, "You look good on the outside, but on the inside, you're full of dead men's bones." Jesus came to clarify what the Pharisees thought they knew better than everyone else. The world's logic says to hate your enemies but kingdom logic says, 'love your enemies'! The kingdom of God is full of principles and paradoxes that challenge conventional thinking, and sometimes even common sense. But His kingdom and all that it entails holds precedent over every other thing!

The Bible records an incredible promise where the kingdom of God is concerned; "Seek first the kingdom of God, and His righteousness, and all these things will be added unto you." It's clear that when we make the most important thing, the most important thing, everything else in life will fall into proper perspective! There's a lot of people out there today who don't understand the kingdom. They have the same problem as the Pharisees; they know what the Word says, they don't know what it means! As you read your Bible seek to understand the kingdom and you'll not only know what the Bible says, you'll also know what it means! And, consequentially as you grow in your understanding of the kingdom, you'll better understand the Word!

While there are a number of good books out there on the kingdom of God, I would wholeheartedly recommend these few as they have profoundly impacted me at a deep level and helped me with my understanding of the kingdom.

- *Cosmic Initiative* - Jack Taylor
- *The Unshakable Kingdom and the Unchanging Person* - E. Stanley Jones
- *Rediscovering the Kingdom* - Myles Munroe

LEARNING TO LOOK FOR JESUS

"Every word of the Bible rings with Christ."

—Martin Luther

"Christocentric is a doctrinal term within Christianity, describing theological positions that focus on Jesus Christ as it places its doctrine of justification by grace, which is primarily a Christological doctrine, at the center of its thought. The Christocentric principle is also commonly used for biblical hermeneutics" (Wikipedia).

The Bible can be explained in many different ways but to simplify, it is a Book about Jesus! You might innocently say, "Now, wait a minute!", "Jesus didn't show up until the New Testament!" That's a fair observation, no question about it. But, When you learn that, even in the Old Testament, Jesus is seen in types, shadows, imagery, and symbolism. It's then that you begin to understand that He can be found (and should be looked for!) throughout all of Scripture.

In fact when God, the Creator, made man His exact words were, "Let Us make man in Our image." There was total agreement, synchronization, and cooperation at that moment between the Father, The Son, Jesus, and the Holy Spirit. Even though Jesus was not in 'bodily form' at the time of creation, He was there!

So, what does it mean to be Christocentric? For starters, let's remember to keep Jesus at the center of everything we read and study. As the passage below states, He should be given the place of preeminence (the fact of surpassing or having superiority over all others) It could also mean that all our reading, studying and teaching is done with Jesus in mind.

He is the image of the invisible God, the firstborn over all creation. For by Him all things were created that are in heaven and that are on earth, visible and invisible, whether thrones or dominions or principalities or powers. All things were created through Him and for Him. And He is before all things, and in Him, all things consist. And He is the head of the body, the church, who is the beginning, the firstborn from the dead, that in all things He may have the preeminence.

Col 1:15-18

How does my understanding of a certain Scripture line up, and mesh, with Jesus' life and His message? That's a question we could pose to ourselves as we are studying the Bible. Christocentric theology makes Jesus the central theme whether you're reading Old Testament or New.

By God's own design, Jesus is to have the preeminence, or superiority in all matters, thoughts, and concerns. When you're reading and studying your Bible remember to keep Jesus at the forefront of your thought. Look for Him in everything you read, and you'll find Him.

In my own preaching and teaching, because of the insight, He has given me personally about the Father, I refer to and talk about the Father a lot. I think it's very important. So, in putting this in the Christocentric context, one must ask himself this question: "Is preaching and teaching from a Christocentric position only preaching and teaching about Jesus? Or is it preaching and teaching the things that Jesus taught?" Obviously, one could easily see that it's both! And, again obviously, Jesus talked a lot about the Father!

Paul, the apostle, had a very unique perspective on it all and in the verse below he touted his own take on the subject of being Christocentric! We should intently take note!

And I, brethren, when I came to you, did not come with excellence of speech or of wisdom declaring to you the testimony of God. For I determined not to know anything among you except Jesus Christ and Him crucified.

1 Cor 2:1-3

DON'T TIE THE ENDS UP!

"In a time of drastic change, it is the learners who inherit the future. The learned find themselves equipped to live in a world which no longer exists."

—Eric Hoffer

It's one of the most important things to learn if you plan to be a lifetime learner, especially in reading and understanding the Bible. And, from 30 years of observation, it's one of the things that seems to be an issue for just about everyone. It's especially a monumental challenge for those having grown up in traditional, conservative, denominational churches.

It's the idea of learning something in Scripture and then logging that in your mind as the Truth. That's not a problem, in and of itself, but it's nearly always true that what you've learned is not "all" of the truth. Religious people are the worst I've ever seen in doing this. They make their mind up that this is just the way it is and close their mind on anything new. It's a problem of monumental proportions! It causes one to become rigid in what he knows or at least thinks he knows. Nearly always the next step is to become intolerant of anyone's perspective that differs from your own. This is one of the primary reasons that there are 4000 denominations out there today!

When you "tie the ends up" you have decided that you know all the truth about a certain subject and refuse to allow any more input on that subject. This is so serious! In fact, if you're not careful, you'll cut off even the Holy Spirit's attempts to bring you into deeper truth. When you tie the ends up, the things you know, or at least think you know, can keep you from other things that you need to know! When you learn things, always keep your mind open to new light on the subject. It's an important part of the Holy Spirit's job to lead us into all Truth. He will definitely do His part. Your job is to, "not tie the ends up!" Remain flexible, pliable and teachable. As you do that, you'll be extending the boundaries of your understanding.

SECTION 2

GETTING THE MOST OUT OF
READING YOUR BIBLE
FOR ALL IT'S WORTH

Get Acquainted With It

Thumb through it. Check out the chapter titles. Don't skip the historical information. You'll find some amazing facts about how the Bible was supernaturally protected and preserved throughout the generations. You'll see how instrumental it has been in the development of our nation as well as how it has profoundly impacted the lives of many historical figures.

Don't Hurry Through It

In all actuality, you could easily read through the whole book in an hour or two. My advice is, "Don't! Slow down!" Take your time. Spend plenty of time on the 'Engage' sections. Get your Bible out and do the exercises. The principles and tips are communicated in such simplicity that you won't have any difficulty understanding them. In a short time, the study principles will become second nature for you, and you'll soon find yourself using them without even thinking about them.

Keep It Handy

Carry it with you as a companion to your Bible, so you can refer to it from time to time when you need to. You'll find it to be helpful when you're reading and studying. Maybe you should carry a few extras with you to give as gifts to someone you want to bless. You'll never know how it might change someone's life!

Teach Someone The Principles You Have Learned

It's a proven fact that when we teach someone else, we are the ones that end up learning the most. I advise you to do that. It'll sharpen you up, and you'll get proficient in your study of the Bible. You might even volunteer to lead a class in your church. If I were your pastor that would make me happy!

Start a Small Group

I'm a huge proponent of small groups for a lot of good reasons. One of the best ways to learn is to get together with friends and discuss a chapter of the book. You might want to do this once a week over an entire year taking time to learn the principles thoroughly. Make it a priority to encourage interaction from everyone in your group. You'll be developing deep interpersonal relationships as well as growing in the Word together.

Read It Again

It's a book that you will be able to draw from continually. Even after you've finished the book and are familiar with the principles thumb through the pages and reread some of the chapters. All the while you'll be solidifying and honing your study skills as well as learning your way around the Bible.

PUT YOURSELF IN THE STORY

"Some books are to be tasted, others to be swallowed, and some few to be chewed and digested."

—Francis Bacon

One of the ways I have found extremely helpful in my study of the Bible is to put myself in the story. By that, I mean to slow down and pretend you are there! Look at the story from the perspective of anyone, or everyone who is in that particular story. For instance, how would the common rank and file of the people of Jerusalem have seen and understood the crucifixion of Jesus? Pretend you're one of them in the crowd. What would the Roman soldiers have been thinking? What would the close followers of Jesus have thought about it? If you were there on the road to the cross, what would you have thought? All these questions can become eye openers for you if you'll put yourself in the story. When you do this, remember to take into consideration the customs, practices, and mindsets of that particular time. Your perspective will broaden, and you'll have a much deeper understanding of what might have been happening.

If you'll develop this practice, you'll find yourself enjoying the Bible much more!

RENEWING YOUR MIND

"It's what we think we know already that prevents us from learning."

—Claude Bernar

And do not be conformed to this world, but be transformed by the renewing of your mind, that you may prove what is that good and acceptable and perfect will of God.

Rom 12:2

At every opening of your Bible, you have the awesome opportunity to "renew your mind"! In Paul's letter to the Romans, he issued a warning and an encouragement to the saints there. "Don't be conformed to this world." It's a subtle thing that happens to us, and if we don't do something to offset it, it will sink its claws in us. The world, and how the world thinks, has a conforming effect. The Bible states that "you are in the world, but you're not of the world." So, we're going to be surrounded by concepts, mindsets, and opinions that may be far from Biblical values but that we've accepted and have lived much our lives from that understanding. For us to be true spiritual beings, as the Father has intended, we must have our minds renewed according to His Word.

As you read and study your Bible, you are allowing the truths to pervade your mind. And, when you happen onto those truths, you must allow them to replace any untruths, or partial truths, in favor of Biblical truth. The more you do this, the more your mind will be renewed according to what eternal truth actually is, and the Holy Spirit will lead you into all Truth.

You might ask why this is so important. Your thinking, and subsequently your behavior, is based on your perception of truth, or the things that you believe. If you're like me, you may realize that many of the things we believed and accepted as truth dim in the light of Biblical truth. When we take Paul's advice and allow Biblical truth to "renew our mind" we find ourselves being changed from the inside out. We discover that we now think totally different about some things, which in turn has the incredible power to change our behavior. Even though God deeply desires that for us He doesn't force it on us. Ultimately it's totally up to us. The wise person learns and heeds Biblical truth while inviting it to challenge what he thinks he knows in favor of what's really true! That's how your mind gets made new!

ENGAGE:

After you've prayed and asked the Holy Spirit for His help, open your Bible to your desired place. As you slowly read, being sensitive to the Holy Spirit's leading, take note of anything that challenges your current patterns of thought. Stop there, meditate on that point and allow it to take the place, or change previously accepted truths. Make note of your new perspective and begin to think and practice this 'new' position in your daily affairs. By doing this, you'll always be renewing (making new!) your mind!

BE A LEARNER

"When you think you know it all, you're as smart as you're ever going to get."

—Cliff Taylor

My dad, Cliff Taylor, gave my brother Monty and I some profound advice growing up; "When you think you know it all, you're as smart as you're ever going to get." If you think about that it proves to be true whether you're a plumber, a doctor or an astronaut, ...or a student of the Bible. I had no idea that little piece of advice would cause me to be a "learner" my whole life. It has made my life much more enjoyable and interesting!

If we're going to be skillful in reading, studying or communicating the Bible in the future then committing to the Father's plan for our lives requires us to be "learners." He has us in the "school of life." Every incident, every event has potential value for us as believers. As we mature, we learn that even the obstacles, challenges and trials have a unique way of forming and shaping us into the image of Jesus. We begin to understand that the Father has an intricate, detailed, plan for our life. We can also learn not to take ourselves too seriously. As we do that, we can laugh at our mistakes, learn from them, and move on!

Paul, the apostle, took a similar position; "I don't count myself as having attained (arrived)." He had learned a lot. He was an authority on the grace of God. He was known in several nations as the 'go-to' guy for the revelation and questions about Jesus and the kingdom of God. He knew a lot, but he didn't let it go to his head. As a result of that mindset, he remained a 'learner' until his last breath. When you open your Bible to read, prepare to learn. Keep your heart and mind open to the direction and insight that the Holy Spirit gives. There are plenty of people out there in the church today who act as if they have it "all knowed up," when it comes to the Bible. But they've stopped growing. Learners are always growing. They never stop. Learners never get bored. Life is always exciting! I'd like to be like Paul; to "run the good race," "fight the good fight" and die learning!

You can decide today to be a learner. I think you should. Your life will be exponentially better and more exciting if you will decide now to be a learner.

"GOOD GROUND"

"Who speaks for God? He does quite nicely for Himself. Through His holy and infallible Word and the quiet obedience of His servants."

—Charles Colson

In the parable of the "sower and the soils," in Matthew, Mark, and Luke each of the writers of the Good News talks about "good ground." The seed, which is the Word of God, can have a powerful effect on the readers of Scripture. That seed can bring forth an immeasurable amount of wisdom when it falls on good ground. The parable goes into detail on what happens when the ground is not good. "Some seeds fell by the wayside, and the birds came and devoured it." This could be described as elements of truth that one might not have readily received at the moment and over time, because it wasn't totally received or adhered to, the truth dissipated away. "Some seeds fell in stony places, where they did not have much earth; they immediately sprang up, but when the sun came up they were scorched because they had no root they withered away." "Stony places" could be described as someone who is "hard," or even unbelieving of spiritual truth. And, "where there was not much earth," could easily be interpreted as someone who has only a little depth of maturity and understanding.

"Some fell among thorns, and the thorns sprang up and choked them." The "thorns" could be the thousands of bits of information and concepts that we have accepted as truth but actually can't stand up in the light of Biblical truth. I've seen it happen; someone hears and receives some actual Truth but the pressure of the world's thinking forces one back into believing half-truths, and in many cases—flat out lies!

"But, some seeds fell on good ground and brought forth much fruit." It's interesting to note that both Mark and Luke recorded that some seeds yielded a harvest of thirty, sixty and some even a hundredfold. But, Matthew saw it quite differently. He said that "some of the seed fell on good ground and brought forth fruit, some hundred, some sixty and some thirty-fold." I have an opinion that you might want to consider. Matthew was a tax collector. Hated and despised by everyone, it's totally possible that the only time he felt valued by anyone was when Jesus walked by and said, "Follow Me." He did that, and as they say, the rest is history! But the difference could be that Matthew didn't have any religious baggage to stand in the way of him receiving eternal truths. And, while each of these men's story about the good ground was positive, Matthew saw it, I believe, from the Lord's perspective the clearest!

So, if we're going to get the most out of what we read in the Bible, just what is it that constitutes 'good ground'? I would describe good ground in several ways. Good ground would be a clean heart—one with pure motives. It is a heart that desires the pure truth no matter how alien it might be to them at the moment. It's a heart that's willing to believe by faith and willing to change and adapt. A clean heart is open to Biblical truth challenging how they think, a heart that allows the truth to change their behavior. It's a heart that, above all, wants to know the Truth, and God's will for his life.

Of all that farmers do including plowing, sowing, fertilizing, waiting and harvesting the one thing that's more productive than anything else is getting the ground prepared before the seed is planted. The ground has to be in good shape to plan for a good harvest. It might even take longer than some of the other things that farmers do, but the principle is simple: If the ground is not in good shape it's going to adversely affect the harvest in a big, big way!

On the other hand, if you want to experience a hundred-fold blessing on what you read and study, get the ground ready! You're the only one who can make sure that the seed falls on good ground!

READING BY FAITH

"True faith rests upon the character of God and asks no further proof than the moral perfections of the One who cannot lie. It is enough that God has said it."

—A.W. Tozer

When we read the Bible, we're able to trust its contents for several valid reasons. First, it has miraculously stood the test of time. Amidst many calculated and well-planned campaigns throughout history to destroy the Bible, it's still around. The Father, Himself, has seen to it that His Word would be preserved no matter how strong or determined the opposition to it might be. It'll still be around generations after we're gone if the Lord tarries in His coming.

We are able to understand and comprehend the Truth of the Bible because we've been blessed with an extremely high quality of faith. Romans 3 says that we have all been dealt "the measure of faith." Our faith probably has much more potential than any of us can imagine, much less than we walk in. We have been given this measure of His faith to fulfill His entire plan for our lives no matter how grandiose that might seem. Whatever the task, whatever the challenge, whatever the obstacle, we have adequate faith to navigate them all.

When we read the Bible, we must read it and receive the Truth contained therein by faith. There's no other way to get the most out of the Word. The stories of the parting of the Red Sea to the ones of those being raised from the dead or stories of the miracle birth of Jesus to His glorious resurrection, all must be received, and believed, by faith.

A while back, the Spirit of the Lord spoke to me in that still, small voice, "Don't complicate, with logic, that which can only be understood by faith." The Bible is loaded with incredible principles, events, and stories. We must read it by faith if we're going to get the most out of it.

MARK IT UP! BE A NOTETAKER!

"Acquiring the habit of note-taking is a wonderfully complementary skill to that of listening."

—Richard Branson

Hopefully, you've already made the decision to be a lifetime learner. Great choice; smart decision! There are those out there who already think they know it all when it comes to the Bible but they're not growing anymore.

One of the most practical things that has helped me in my own journey of learning to read the Bible is to be a notetaker. I don't remember anyone instructing me to start taking notes but I've been doing it since the very beginning of my Bible reading experience, and I can easily say it's helped me considerably. It's a proven fact in educational psychology that when you write something down, you have a much better chance of remembering it. It helps to establish it in your mind. So, in my preaching and teaching being able to remember what I've read, where it's located and how it's used has been extremely helpful for me. In my office at home, I have no less than 20-25 yellow and white legal pads completely full of notes. Some of those legal pads are 25 years or older. They're full of things that I thought were important at the time. There are literally hundreds of words and verses that I have written down what the Lord was saying to me through them and what I was learning at the time. I can confidently say I've never thrown a single one of them away. No way! The things I have written down were far too important to throw away. I always thought that I'd go back, reread them and refer to them often to review or refresh but that hasn't been the case. I'm sure it would be productive, and I still may do it, but so far the value in taking all those notes for me has been that they have helped me to learn and to remember.

Anytime I hear someone preach or teach, I'm taking notes, lots of them. Anytime I've having one of those intense kingdom conversations in my office with my closest friends, I'm taking notes! Anytime I hear an important comment or quote from someone, I'm taking notes! Anytime I have a guest speaker in my church. I'm taking notes! Anytime I read and study the Bible I'm taking notes! Anytime I wake up in the middle of the night with a scripture or a thought; I'm taking notes! Anytime during the day, whether I'm with someone or just driving down the highway and the Holy Spirit gets my attention about something, I'm taking notes! (careful when driving! LOL) You get it? I'm a notetaker, and it's clearly been one of the best habits I've ever taken on. You should do it, starting now!

I'm also an avid "marker-upper" of my Bible! On over half the pages in the Bible I'm currently using there are notes in the margins on either side; notes in the center margins; notes and marks in the actual body of the text itself. I had a friend once tell me that he never writes on the pages of his Bible. "Why?", I asked. "Because it's a holy book and shouldn't be tampered with or defaced." Hmm. Well, if that's true, I'm in deep, deep trouble! Just kidding, but to each his own. If you don't think you ought to mark in your Bible, don't. But as for me and my house … we're gonna mark it up!

I should also add here that as a pastor, teacher and leader nothing blesses me much more in a service than to look out in the audience and seeing people taking notes. It says to me that this person is engaged. It says that they're serious about what's being communicated. It says that they are placing enough importance in what they're hearing that they don't want to forget it. Note taking is a surefire way not to let those things slip off into oblivion!

A word of warning and encouragement: You will often have that brilliant thought of something noteworthy, something you know you never want to forget. You'll think at that moment that you'll remember that thought forever. You might even plan to write it down as soon as you get a little free time. I know from experience that when I have those, sometimes fleeting, thoughts that I need to write them down immediately so that they're not lost forever!

Take your pen with you to church. Write those important things down, and if it's OK with you, mark that Bible up with some colored pencils or highlighters. Take some good notes; make it a habit. I promise you'll be glad you did.

BE A SEARCHER

"Truth does not change because it is, or is not, believed by a majority of the people."

—Giordano Bruno

As was Paul's custom, when he arrived in Berea, a city in northern Greece, he and Silas went straight to the synagogue of the Jews. He did this in nearly every place he went. At the synagogue, he would reason with them from the Scriptures. (the Law and the prophets since there was at that time no New Testament as we know it today) He started with them on "common ground," things that they mutually agreed upon. He would talk to them about the things he knew about the Law. He would point out to them how even the Old Covenant writings pointed to Jesus. He would eventually get to Jesus, His life, His teachings and then His death, burial, and resurrection. That's where most of the Jews "got off the bus." More often than not they rejected the teaching. The self-righteous Jews exercised their indignation toward Paul by throwing him out of the synagogue. They were so infuriated on more than one occasion that they beat him brutally. So bad in fact that on at least one occasion that they left him on the road, for dead.

But, the Bereans were different. They were accepting of Paul and open to this new teaching about Jesus. Acts 17 recalls that account, "They received the word with all readiness, and searched the Scriptures daily to find out whether these things were so." They kept an open heart to the controversial things that Paul taught. It was completely off the map of what they thought and believed, but still, they listened intently. They were hungry for Truth, and even though it challenged them on every front they continued to pursue! But, the Bereans didn't just buy into everything Paul said without first searching the Scriptures to find out if what he was saying was true.

It's an admirable trait. One of the great ways to grow in the Lord is to sit under good teaching. There's a lot of great Bible teachers out there. We should seek them out and listen to what they have to say. But, we should be like the Bereans; we should have an open heart, listen well and diligently search the Scriptures, personally, to see for sure if what they're teaching can stand up to the Truth of the Bible.

When Luke penned the words to the book of Acts, he commended the Berean believers. It was a good thing they were doing. So, in the process of hearing the Word of God and developing your understanding of the Truth, be like the Bereans. Be a Searcher!

ENGAGE:

The next time you are listening to a Christian speaker make a note or two to check up on what you heard him say. Start to make it a practice of doing this and you'll be developing a habit that produces a twofold benefit:

1) You'll be learning to 'test' the Word that you hear like the Bereans did. And as you grow, you'll be able to detect error if, or when, it might occur.

2) Anytime you search the Word like this you'll be learning much more about it. By doing this, you are speeding up the process of your spiritual maturity.

BE A DOER

"Ultimate value comes not in reading but in applying truth."
—Gary Chapman

"Faith without works is dead"! James encouraged the readers of his short letter to "be doers of the Word, and not hearers only." He concludes that thought by saying that one who does that will be blessed in all that he does.

You're probably not reading this book if you're not serious about learning from the Bible. When we read the Word, we learn lots of practical principles that we can easily apply to our lives. The Holy Spirit's guidance and illumination cause the Word to come alive in us. It can become, in us, a powerful force that directs our entire lives. The Bible even says of itself that it is "quick" (alive), and "powerful"! As that happens, we find ourselves with the potential to be "agents of change" in the world. We're armed and dangerous, so to speak. Armed with the Truth that the world is looking for, whether they know it or not; armed with the Holy Spirit Who directs us at every turn and reveals God's will for us in every situation; armed with love, the agape kind, that never fails! We're ambassadors of the kingdom of God, and we're here on the planet to fulfill our God-given destiny to make the world a better place and to show the world Who God really is!

Yes, we all have that potential. But, unless we put our hand to the plow, as the Word encourages, we're taking a chance of missing our destiny. You were created for signs and wonders! All things are possible for you, and nothing is impossible; You can do all things through Christ, Who strengthens you! You've been given "all things" that pertain to life and godliness! You have an abundance of resources for every good work! You don't have to do any of this under your own power but under the power of God! Jesus said if we believed in Him and the works that He did, we would do those works as well. He takes it to a revolutionary level when He says, "And even greater works than these will you do because I go to the Father." That's some kind of mandate!

When we read and study the Word we can just soak up the knowledge, and there's no doubt about it, we'll be better human beings because of it. But, we can decide now to be "doers" of the Word and watch the supernatural power of God at work through us! Incidentally, the quicker you can use the Word that you have learned, the better! In that way, the Word becomes Life!

In the final analysis, it doesn't really matter how much you know, but how much of the truth you walk in! I encourage you to be a "doer of the Word!"

ENGAGE:

Read Proverbs 3:5-6:

Trust in the Lord with all your heart, and lean not on your own understanding; in all your ways acknowledge Him, and He will direct your paths.

Think of something practical going on in your life at this moment that might require prayer or extra attention. Start by inviting the Lord into the middle of that situation. Let Him know (vocally) that you are looking to Him for wisdom and guidance in that area. Listen, be patient and be watching for ways that He answers your prayer in this area. By doing this, you are developing a pattern for inviting Him into every area of your life. In the future when you happen onto new truths ask the Spirit for ways or "open doors" to put that Word to practical use. The quicker you put to use the things you learn, the better. That way the Word becomes "life!" Before you know it, you'll become a "doer," and not just a "hearer," of the Word!

SECTION 3

A BRIEF HISTORY

How did we come to have the Bible?

"In the beginning was the Word, and the Word was with God, and the Word was God. He was in the beginning with God. All things were made through Him, and without Him, nothing was made that was made. In Him was life, and the life was the light of men. And the light shines in the darkness, and the darkness did not comprehend it."

John 1:1-5

Of course, you understand that the "written" Word was 'not' in the beginning! Many people make the honest mistake of thinking the Bible is saying that in this passage. Not true. A closer reading of the verses reveal that John is not writing about a document (the Bible) at all, which would actually come along much later, but referring to Jesus, the Living Word. I think it's important in learning how to glean the most from your Bible reading that, ultimately, the Bible is a book about Jesus! While there are hundreds of important Bible characters, all of which are significant to the overall picture, everything points to, and hinges on Him! He IS the Word, the Living Word!

In ancient Old Testament times, no one had the written Word except the priests. It was their responsibility to relay to the people what God was saying … and what His appointed people were saying and doing. There are at least thirty-six different authors in the Bible, who wrote in three continents and many countries, during a period of fifteen hundred years. Down through the generations, beginning with Moses God's words, His plan, His ways, and His motives were recorded. Whether on tablets of stone, on papyrus (paper) or otherwise, God made sure that these things were remembered and written down for all the generations that would follow. As evidenced by the verse below the Holy Spirit guided God's spokesmen to say, to do and to write the details of the Book. The Holy Spirit would emphasize 'only' the things that were important to the Father!

… no prophecy of Scripture is of any private interpretation, for prophecy never came by the will of man, but holy men of God spoke as they were moved by the Holy Spirit.

2 Peter 1:20-21

The Bible is a collection of sacred texts or scriptures that are a product of divine inspiration and a record of the relationship between God and humans. Within the pages of the Bible God reveals His plan of redemption for all mankind. With estimated total sales of over 5 billion copies, the Bible is widely considered to be the most influential and best-selling book of all time.

When you look at the history and timeline of how the Bible was miraculously preserved down through the generations you will gain a much greater respect for "it," and for the incredible God we have that assures us it would never be lost nor diluted!

History of the Bible Timeline

2000 BC - 200 BC

Creation - B.C. 2000 - Originally, the earliest Scriptures are handed down from generation to generation orally.

Circa B.C. 2000-1500 - The book of Job, perhaps the oldest book of the Bible, is written.

Circa B.C. 1500-1400 - The stone tablets of the Ten Commandments are given to Moses at Mount Sinai and later stored in the Ark of the Covenant.

Circa B.C. 1400–400 - The manuscripts comprising the original Hebrew Bible (39 Old Testament books) are completed. The Book of the Law is kept in the tabernacle and later in the Temple beside the Ark of the Covenant.

Circa B.C. 300 - All of the original Old Testament Hebrew books have been written, collected, and recognized as official, canonical books.

Circa B.C. 250–200 - The Septuagint, a popular Greek translation of the Hebrew Bible (39 Old Testament books), is produced. The 14 books of the Apocrypha are also included.

1 AD - 500 AD

Circa A.D. 45–100 - Original 27 books of the Greek New Testament are written.

Circa A.D. 140-150 - Marcion of Sinope's heretical "New Testament" prompted Orthodox Christians to establish a New Testament canon.

Circa A.D. 200 - The Jewish Mishnah, the Oral Torah, is first recorded.

Circa A.D. 240 - Origen compiles the Hexapla, a six-columned parallel of Greek and Hebrew texts.

Circa A.D. 305-310 - Lucian of Antioch's Greek New Testament text becomes the basis for the Textus Receptus.

Circa A.D. 312 - Codex Vaticanus is possibly among the original 50 copies of the Bible ordered by Emperor Constantine. It is eventually kept in the Vatican Library in Rome.

A.D. 367 - Athanasius of Alexandria identifies the complete New Testament canon (27 books) for the first time.

A.D. 382-384 - Saint Jerome translates the New Testament from original Greek into Latin. This translation becomes part of the Latin Vulgate manuscript.

A.D. 397 - Third Synod of Carthage approves the New Testament canon (27 books).

A.D. 390-405 - Saint Jerome translates the Hebrew Bible into Latin and completes the Latin Vulgate manuscript. It includes the 39 Old Testament books, 27 New Testament books, and 14 Apocrypha books.

A.D. 500 - By now the Scriptures have been translated into multiple languages, not limited to but including an Egyptian version (Codex Alexandrinus), a Coptic version, an Ethiopic translation, a Gothic version (Codex Argenteus), and an Armenian version. Some consider the Armenian to be the most beautiful and accurate of all ancient translations.

501 AD - 950 AD

A.D. 600 - The Roman Catholic Church declares Latin as the only language for Scripture.

A.D. 680 - Caedmon, English poet and monk, renders Bible books and stories into Anglo Saxon poetry and song.

A.D. 735 - Bede, English historian and monk, translates the Gospels into Anglo Saxon.

A.D. 775 - The Book of Kells, a richly decorated manuscript containing the Gospels and other writings, is completed by Celtic monks in Ireland.

Circa A.D. 865 - Saints Cyril and Methodius begin translating the Bible into Old Church Slavonic.

A.D. 950 - The Lindisfarne Gospels manuscript is translated into Old English.

995 AD - 1500 AD

Circa A.D. 995-1010 - Aelfric, an English abbot, translates parts of Scripture into Old English.

A.D. 1205 - Stephen Langton, theology professor and later Archbishop of Canterbury, creates the first chapter divisions in the books of the Bible.

A.D. 1229 - Council of Toulouse strictly forbids and prohibits lay people from owning a Bible.

A.D. 1240 - French Cardinal Hugh of Saint Cher publishes the first Latin Bible with the chapter divisions that still exist today. The first division of the Bible into chapters and verses is attributed to Stephen Langton, Archbishop of Canterbury in the 12th century. These chapter divisions were first used by the Jews in 1330 for the Hebrew Old Testament in a manuscript and a printed edition in 1516. This system of chapter divisions likewise came into the Greek manuscripts of the New Testament in the 1400s. It was Robert Stephanus, a French book printer, whose versification of the Bible has prevailed to the present. He took over the verse divisions already indicated in the Hebrew Bible and assigned numbers to them within the chapter divisions already assigned by Langton. While riding on horseback from Paris to Lyons, he affixed his own verse divisions to the New Testament and numbered them within Langton's chapter divisions.

A.D. 1325 - English hermit and poet, Richard Rolle de Hampole, and English poet William Shoreham translate the Psalms into metrical verse.

Circa A.D. 1330 - Rabbi Solomon ben Ismael first places chapter divisions in the margins of the Hebrew Bible.

A.D. 1381-1382 - John Wycliffe and associates, in defiance of the organized Church, believing that people should be permitted to read the Bible in their own language, begin to translate and produce the first handwritten manuscripts of the entire Bible in English. These include the 39 Old Testament books, 27 New Testament books, and 14 Apocrypha books.

A.D. 1388 - John Purvey revises Wycliffe's Bible.

A.D. 1415 - 31 years after Wycliffe's death, the Council of Constance charges him with more than 260 counts of heresy.

A.D. 1428 - 44 years after Wycliffe's death, church officials dig up his bones, burn them, and scatter the ashes on Swift River.

A.D. 1455 - After the invention of the printing press in Germany, Johannes Gutenberg produces the first printed Bible, the Gutenberg Bible, in the Latin Vulgate.

1501 AD - 2001 AD

A.D. 1516 - Desiderius Erasmus produces a Greek New Testament, forerunner to the Textus Receptus.

A.D. 1517 - Daniel Bomberg's Rabbinic Bible contains the first printed Hebrew version (Masoretic text) with chapter divisions.

A.D. 1522 - Martin Luther translates and publishes the New Testament for the first time into German from the 1516 Erasmus version.

A.D. 1524 - Bomberg prints a second edition Masoretic text prepared by Jacob ben Chayim.

A.D. 1525 - William Tyndale produces the first translation of the New Testament from Greek into English.

A.D. 1527 - Erasmus publishes a fourth edition Greek-Latin translation.

A.D. 1530 - Jacques Lefèvre d'Étaples completes the first French language translation of the entire Bible.

A.D. 1535 - Myles Coverdale's Bible completes Tyndale's work, producing the first complete printed Bible in the English language. It includes the 39 Old Testament books, 27 New Testament books, and 14 Apocrypha books.

A.D. 1536 - Martin Luther translates the Old Testament into the commonly-spoken dialect of the German people, completing his translation of the entire Bible in German.

A.D. 1536 - Tyndale is condemned as a heretic, strangled, and burned at the stake.

A.D. 1537 - The Matthew Bible (commonly known as the Matthew-Tyndale Bible), a second complete printed English translation, is published, combining the works of Tyndale, Coverdale and John Rogers.

A.D. 1539 - The Great Bible, the first English Bible authorized for public use, is printed.

A.D. 1546 - Roman Catholic Council of Trent declares the Vulgate as the exclusive Latin authority for the Bible.

A.D. 1553 - Robert Estienne publishes a French Bible with chapter and verse divisions. This system of numbering becomes widely accepted and is still found in most Bible's today.

A.D. 1560 - The Geneva Bible is printed in Geneva, Switzerland. It is translated by English refugees and published by John Calvin's brother-in-law, William Whittingham. The Geneva Bible is the first English Bible to add numbered verses to the chapters. It becomes the Bible of the Protestant Reformation, more popular than the 1611 King James Version for decades after its original release.

A.D. 1568 - The Bishop's Bible, a revision of the Great Bible, is introduced in England to compete with the popular but "inflammatory toward the institutional Church" Geneva Bible.

A.D. 1582 - Dropping its 1,000-year-old Latin-only policy, the Church of Rome produces the first English Catholic Bible, the Rheims New Testament, from the Latin Vulgate.

A.D. 1592 - The Clementine Vulgate (authorized by Pope Clementine VIII), a revised version of the Latin Vulgate, becomes the authoritative Bible of the Catholic Church.

A.D. 1609 - The Douay Old Testament is translated into English by the Church of Rome, to complete the combined Douay-Rheims Version.

A.D. 1611 - The King James Version, also called the "Authorized Version" of the Bible is published. It is said to be the most printed book in the history of the world, with more than one billion copies in print.

A.D. 1663 - John Eliot's Algonquin Bible is the first Bible printed in America, not in English, but in the native Algonquin Indian language.

A.D. 1782 - Robert Aitken's Bible is the first English language (KJV) Bible printed in America.

A.D. 1790 - Matthew Carey publishes a Roman Catholic Douay-Rheims Version English Bible in America.

A.D. 1790 - William Young prints the first pocket-sized "school edition" King James Version Bible in America.

A.D. 1791 - The Isaac Collins Bible, the first family Bible (KJV), is printed in America.

A.D. 1791 - Isaiah Thomas prints the first illustrated Bible (KJV) in America.

A.D. 1808 - Jane Aitken (daughter of Robert Aitken), is the first woman to print a Bible.

A.D. 1833 - Noah Webster, after publishing his famous dictionary, releases his own revised edition of the King James Bible.

A.D. 1841 - The English Hexapla New Testament, a comparison of the original Greek language and six important English translations, is produced.

A.D. 1844 - The Codex Sinaiticus, a handwritten Koine Greek manuscript of both Old and New Testament texts dating back to the fourth century, is rediscovered by German Bible scholar Konstantin Von Tischendorf in the Monastery of Saint Catherine on Mount Sinai.

A.D. 1881-1885 - The King James Bible is revised and published as the Revised Version (RV) in England.

A.D. 1901 - The American Standard Version, the first major American revision of the King James Version, is published.

A.D. 1946-1952 - The Revised Standard Version is published.

A.D. 1947-1956 - The Dead Sea Scrolls are discovered.

A.D. 1971 - The New American Standard Bible (NASB) is published.

A.D. 1973 - The New International Version (NIV) is published.

A.D. 1982 - The New King James Version (NKJV) is published.

A.D. 1986 - The discovery of the Silver Scrolls, believed to be the oldest Bible text ever, is announced. They were found three years earlier in the Old City of Jerusalem by Gabriel Barkay of Tel Aviv University.

A.D. 1996 - The New Living Translation (NLT) is published.

A.D. 2001 - The English Standard Version (ESV) is published.

The Gutenberg Bible

It is a beautiful fact that the first book in the world print with movable types was the Bible. About 180 copies were printed by Johannes Gutenberg, inventor of the printing press. It took three years to do it, from 1453-1456. The Gutenberg Bibles were copied from a manuscript of the Vulgate translation and was printed in Latin.

Only about 50 copies have been located, many of them in poor condition. One copy, printed on vellum and said to be one of the three perfect copies made, is owned by the Library of Congress and obtained for $400,000.

For anyone interested, a well-preserved two-volume set of the Gutenberg edition is on sale in New York City for $3.2 million.

Sources: Willmington's Bible Handbook, www.greatsite.com, Crossway; Bible Museum, Biblica; Christianity Today, and Theopedia.

INTERESTING BIBLE FACTS
AND STORIES

"Draw the honey out of the comb of Scripture, and live on its sweetness."
—C.H. Spurgeon

- It takes 70 hours and 40 minutes to read the Bible at pulpit rate.
- It takes 52 hours and 20 minutes to read the Old Testament.
- It takes 18 hours and 20 minutes to read the New Testament.
- In the Old Testament, the Psalms takes the longest to read: 4 hours and 28 minutes.
- In the New Testament, the Gospel of Luke takes 2 hours and 43 minutes (Eleanor Doan).
- The Geneva Bible is the first Bible to use numbered verses. It is also the Bible Shakespeare used and the one that the Pilgrims brought to America in 1620.
- While it took over 1,000 years to write the Old Testament, the New Testament was written within a period of 50-75 years.
- Moses contributed the most books to the Old Testament. He wrote the first five books of the Bible (the Pentateuch).
- The Apostle Paul wrote the most books in the New Testament. Fourteen different books, over half of the New Testament, were written by Paul.
- Nearly 8 in 10 Americans regard the Bible as either the literal word of God or as inspired by God.
- It is estimated that the earliest biblical work, the first five books written by Moses, dates from around 1450 BC although some believe that the book of Job, written by an unknown Israelite, was written around 1500 BC. The most recent book in the Old Testament is Malachi which was written around 400 BC.
- The most recent biblical work (Book of Revelation) dates to around 100 AD (following the death and resurrection of Christ). The newest book in the New Testament is probably the book of James which was written around 45 AD.
- The original works of the Bible were written in three different languages – Hebrew, Aramaic, and Greek.
- Wisest Man in the Bible: Solomon

- Strongest Man in the Bible: Samson
- Bible Translations: Around 1200 languages and dialects
- Number of Books in the Bible: 66
- Number of Books in the Old Testament: 39
- Number of Books in the New Testament: 27
- Number of Chapters in the Bible: 1189
- Number of Chapters in the Old Testament: 929
- Number of Chapters in the New Testament: 260
- Number of Verses in the Bible: 31,173
- Number of Verses in the Old Testament: 23,214
- Number of Verses in the New Testament: 7,959
- Longest Chapter in the Bible: Psalm 119
- Shortest Chapter in the Bible: Psalm 117
- Shortest Verse in the Bible: "Jesus Wept"(John 11:35)
- The Bible is the most shoplifted/stolen book in the world

Standard Equipment on Pony Express

The Pony Express was a thrilling part of early American history. It ran from St Joseph, Missouri, to Sacramento, California—a distance of 1900 miles. The trip was made in ten days. Forty men, each riding 50 miles a day, dashed along the trail on 500 of the best horses the West could provide.

To conserve weight, clothing was very light, saddles were extremely small and thin, and no weapons were carried. The horses themselves wore small shoes or none at all. The mail pouches were flat and very conservative in size. Letters had to be written on thin paper, and postage was $5.00 an ounce (a tremendous sum those days).

Yet, each rider carried a full-sized Bible! It was presented to him when he joined the Pony Express, and he took it with him despite all the scrupulous weight precautions (*Our Daily Bread*).

Oil From Moses's Crib

The fact that the Standard Oil Company discovered oil and is operating wells in Egypt is generally known, but the reason for its going to that ancient land to look for oil is probably not so well-known.

It is asserted that one of the directors of the company happened to read the second chapter of Exodus. The third verse caught his attention. It states that the ark of bulrushes which the mother of Moses made for her child was "daubed with slime and with pitch."

This gentleman reasoned that where there was pitch, there must be oil, and if there was oil in Moses' time, it is probably still there. So the company sent out Charles Whitshott, its geologist and oil expert, to make investigations, with the result that oil was discovered (Chicago Daily News).

Bible Vending Machines

From Brussels, Belgium came this report:

"A vending machine which once dispensed candy and cigarettes here now drops copies of the four gospels when a Belgian ten franc coin (about 20 cents) is inserted.

Just as it once provided customers with a choice of candies, the converted machine now provides a choice in languages. The books are available in French and Dutch.

The director of the Belgian Bible Society placed the machine outside a Bible Society office near a major bus and trolley stop. He reports that about one hundred gospels a month are dispensed through the vending machine."

Bible Reading in Space

A group of Gideons had been meeting each Monday morning for prayer in Pasadena, Texas, a suburb of Houston. One of them confided to the group that he had been praying that God's Word would be aboard the sophisticated craft on its historic mission. Bass Redd, chief of the flight technical branch of the Manned Spacecraft Center, heard the remark and said, "Let me see what I can do. I know Commander Borman. He is a fine Christian. You claim Jeremiah 33:3 ("Call to Me, and I will answer you, and show you great and mighty things, which you do not know.")

In early December the Gideon representative was able to reach Borman and asked, "Do you have a copy of God's Word aboard?" Borman allegedly replied, "No, and I'm glad you reminded me of it."

The Gideons presented all three astronauts with the New Testaments which they took on the journey to the moon.

Commander Borman also took along his personal copy of the Bible. Each edition was covered with noncombustible material. The first ten verses of Genesis 1 were read by the three astronauts on Christmas Eve from Commander Borman's own Bible, passed—or floated—from man to man.

BOOKS OF THE BIBLE

The Old Testament (39)

Genesis
Exodus
Leviticus
Numbers
Deuteronomy
Joshua
Judges
Ruth
1 Samuel
2 Samuel
1 Kings
2 Kings
1 Chronicles
2 Chronicles
Ezra
Nehemiah
Esther
Job
Psalms
Proverbs
Ecclesiastes
Song of Solomon
Isaiah
Jeremiah
Lamentations
Ezekiel
Daniel
Hosea
Joel
Amos
Obadiah
Jonah
Micah
Nahum
Habakkuk
Zephaniah
Haggai
Zechariah
Malachi

The New Testament (27)

Matthew
Mark
Luke
John
Acts (of the Apostles)
Romans
1 Corinthians
2 Corinthians
Galatians
Ephesians
Philippians
Colossians
1 Thessalonians
2 Thessalonians
1 Timothy
2 Timothy
Titus
Philemon
Hebrews
James
1 Peter
2 Peter
1 John
2 John
3 John
Jude
Revelation

THE DIVISIONS OF THE BIBLE

Old Testament - 39 Books

The Pentateuch (Written by Moses)

Genesis
Exodus
Leviticus
Numbers
Deuteronomy

Historical Books

Joshua
Judges
Ruth
I Samuel; II Samuel
I Kings; II Kings (Unknown, but evidence suggests Jeremiah)
I Chronicles; II Chronicles (Thought to be Ezra)
Ezra
Nehemiah
Esther

Books of Wisdom/Poetry

Job
Psalms (Various authors, David being the most prominent)
Proverbs (Various authors, Solomon being the most prominent)
Ecclesiastes (Thought to be Solomon)
Song of Solomon

Major Prophets
(Major & Minor are in reference to the size of the books)

Isaiah
Jeremiah
Lamentations (Author thought to be Jeremiah)
Ezekiel
Daniel

Minor Prophets

Hosea
Joel
Amos
Obadiah
Jonah
Micah
Nahum
Habakkuk
Zephaniah
Haggai
Zechariah
Malachi

New Testament - 27 Books

Gospels

Matthew
Mark
Luke
John

Apostolic History

Acts of the Apostles (Written by Luke)

Paul's Epistles

Romans
I Corinthians
II Corinthians
Galatians
Ephesians
Philippians
Colossians
I Thessalonians
II Thessalonians
I Timothy

II Timothy
Titus
Philemon

Other Epistles

Hebrews (Unknown, possibly Paul)
James
I Peter, II Peter
I John, II John, III John
Jude

Revelation (Authored by John)

WHAT BIBLE AUTHORS SAY ABOUT GOD'S WORD

All Scripture is given by inspiration of God and is profitable for doctrine, for reproof, for correction, for instruction in righteousness, that the man of God may be complete, thoroughly equipped for every good work.

2 Tim 3:16-17

And so we have the prophetic word confirmed, which you do well to heed as a light that shines in a dark place, until the day dawns and the morning star rises in your hearts; knowing this first, that no prophecy of Scripture is of any private interpretation, for prophecy never came by the will of man, but holy men of God spoke as they were moved by the Holy Spirit.

2 Peter 1:19-21

The grass withers, the flower fades, but the Word of God stands forever.
Isaiah 40:8

Man shall not live by bread alone, but by every word that proceeds out of the mouth of God.

Matt 4:4

"Your word is a lamp unto my feet and a light unto my path.
Ps 119:105

For the word of God is living and powerful, and sharper than any two-edged sword, piercing even to the division of soul and spirit, and of joints and marrow, and is a discerner of the thoughts and intents of the heart.

Heb 4:12-13

This is my comfort in my affliction, For Your word has given me life.
Ps 119:50

Before I was afflicted, I went astray, But now I keep Your word.
Ps 119:67

My soul faints for Your salvation, But I hope in Your word.

Ps 119:81

Forever, O Lord, Your word is settled in heaven.

Ps 119:89

You are my hiding place and my shield; I hope in Your word.

Ps 119:114

Direct my steps by Your word, And let no iniquity have dominion over me.

Ps 119:133

I rise before the dawning of the morning, And cry for help; I hope in Your word.

Ps 119:147

The entirety of Your word is truth, And every one of Your righteous judgments endures forever.

Ps 119:160

I rejoice at Your word as one who finds great treasure.

Ps 119:162

By faith, we understand that the worlds were framed by the word of God so that the things which are seen were not made of things which are visible.

Heb 11:3

I have written to you, young men, Because you are strong, and the word of God abides in you, And you have overcome the wicked one.

1 John 2:14

My tongue shall speak of Your word, For all Your commandments are righteousness.

Ps 119:172

"I will worship toward Your holy temple, And praise Your name For Your lovingkindness and Your truth; For You have magnified Your word above all Your name.

Ps 138:2

In the beginning was the Word, and the Word was with God, and the Word was God. He was in the beginning with God. All things were made through Him, and without Him, nothing was made that was made. In Him was life, and the life was the light of men. And the light shines in the darkness, and the darkness did not comprehend it.

John 1:1-5

ENGAGE:

Rather than just skimming through these Bible quotes, don't get in a hurry. Slow down and do a little research into who said them. Find out what they were going through in their personal lives and what might have led to such a profound perspective. As you do this, you'll be developing your own insights and perspective based on what these great Biblical authors have said. Why don't you start to make a few quotes on your perspective of God's Word, yourself?

WHAT "THEY" SAY

"The Bible has stood the test of time because it is divinely inspired by Almighty God, written in ink that cannot be erased by any man, religion, or belief system." —Billy Graham

There have been literally thousands of people, some noteworthy, others completely unknown, who have weighed in on the importance of the Bible. Here's what a few of them have had to say:

"The Bible does not give us a road map for life, but it does give us a compass" —Gordon S. Jackson

"Hear the true Word of God; lay hold of it, and spend your days not in raising hard questions, but in feasting upon precious truth." —C.H. Spurgeon

"The greatest gift you'll ever give your child will be able to teach him to develop the habit of purposely reading, studying, and applying God's Word daily. It will affect every area of his life every day of his life." —Robin Sampson

"The Bible is God's inspired Word - not a mere collection of various opinions, ideas, philosophies, or 'inspired' thoughts." —John MacArthur

"We must allow the Word of God to confront us, to disturb our security, to undermine our complacency and to overthrow our patterns of thought and behavior." —John Stott

"We cannot rely on the doctrine of Scripture until we are absolutely convinced that God is its Author." —John Calvin

"The Bible is the book that makes fools of the wise of this world; it is only understood by the plain and simple-hearted." —Martin Luther

"God has given us His Word to help us make decisions for daily living. The Scriptures are immensely practical, answering many of the questions that haunt us about how we should conduct our lives." —David Hawkins

"The Bible has been one of the greatest motivators of those who believe its content."—Elmer Towns

"God did not give us His Word to satisfy our curiosity but to change our lives." —Charles Swindoll

"Approach God's Word like the divine, supernatural, power-packed text it is." —Beth Moore

"We must allow the Word of God to confront us, to disturb our security, to undermine our complacency and to overthrow our patterns of thought and behavior." —John Stott

The Bible has been instrumental in the forming, shaping and direction of America. Here's what some of our great leaders have said:

"It is impossible to rightly govern the world without God and the Bible." —George Washington

"So great is my veneration of the Bible, that the earlier my children begin to read it the more confident will be my hope that they will prove useful citizens of their country and respectable members of society." —John Quincy Adams

"That book, sir, is the rock on which our republic rests." —Andrew Jackson

"I believe the Bible is the best gift God has ever given to man. All the good from the Savior of the world is communicated to us through this book." —Abraham Lincoln

"It is impossible to mentally or socially enslave a Bible-reading people. The principles of the Bible are the groundwork of human freedom." —Horace Greeley

"I ask every man and woman in this audience that from this day on they will realize that part of the destiny of America lies in their daily perusal of this great Book." —Woodrow Wilson

"Believe, me, sir, never a night goes by, be I ever so tired, but I read the Word of God before I go to bed." —Douglas MacArthur

"The whole of the inspiration of our civilization springs from the teachings of Christ and the lessons of the Prophets. To read the Bible for these fundamentals is a necessity of American life." —Herbert Hoover

"To read the bible is to take a trip to a fair land where the spirit is strengthened, and faith renewed." —Dwight D. Eisenhower

"Hold fast to the Bible as the sheet-anchor of your liberties; write its precepts in your hearts, and practice them in your lives." —Ulysses S. Grant

ENGAGE:

These were just mere men and women, but they saw something profound and life-altering in the Bible. Rather than just reading their quotes and moving on, stop for a few seconds, think about that person and what he/she saw in the Bible. Think about how their perspective influenced their life. When you read their quotes how does what 'they' say influence your own life. Somewhere along the way in your study of the Bible why don't you devise a quote or two of your own as to how this amazing Book has influenced you. Who knows? Your words may profoundly change someone else's life in the future!

WHY YOU CAN TRUST THE AUTHENTICITY OF YOUR BIBLE

"We cannot rely on the doctrine of Scripture until we are absolutely convinced that God is its author."

—John Calvin

All Scripture is given by inspiration of God and is profitable for doctrine, for reproof, for correction, for instruction in righteousness, that the man of God may be complete, thoroughly equipped for every good work.

2 Tim 3:16-17

If we're to believe anything in the Bible, then we should believe everything. It is the foundation of our Christian faith. Both Jesus and the apostles proclaimed that the Bible is the inspired word of God.

When describing the Word of God, there are a few words that are often used to describe its authenticity.

Inerrant - Incapable of being wrong, authoritative, exact, unquestionable, unimpeachable, faultless

Infallible - Incapable of making mistakes, never failing, trustworthy, flawless, reliable, precise, accurate, foolproof

Inspired - As the above verse so clearly indicates, our Bible was divinely inspired by God, Himself.

There are many books written about, and by, various religions. But the Bible is the only one which includes the actual words of God. Those who believe the Bible also believe that God inspired various people through the years to write down His actual words for mankind. The Bible says more than 3,000 times "thus saith the Lord." And the words which follow are quotes from God.

There were several secular historians who also wrote about the events of the New Testament at the same time the Bible was being written. Josephus is the most well-known of them. He was a Jewish historian. Tacitus was a Roman historian who would have no benefit from not telling the truth. Both these men, as well as others, can be used to back up the historical accuracy of the Bible.

There are historical discoveries regularly coming to light that continue to support the accuracy of the Bible. Merrill Unger, who compiled a Bible dictionary wrote, "Old Testament archeology has rediscovered whole nations, resurrected important peoples, and in a most astonishing manner filled in historical gaps, adding immeasurably to the knowledge of Biblical backgrounds."

There are more than 3,200 verses with fulfilled prophecy either within the Bible itself or since the Bible was written. But there are still more than 3,100 verses with unfulfilled prophecies.

Once you deny the inerrancy of the Bible, there's no basis for Biblical teaching. And the power of God is lost because if it's not the Word of God—if what the Bible says is not what God is saying—then how can we preach it with authority and life-transforming ability?

C.S. Lewis, now regarded as one of the great Christian authors of all time, was earlier in life an avowed atheist. At the loss of his mother to cancer and enduring the scorn and pressure from his dad, young Lewis decided there was no God. But the Oxford scholar had a penchant for knowledge and truth. In reading a book by Christian author, George McDonald, Lewis began to be softened to the things of God, and Christianity. Coupled with his friendship with others who were being awakened spiritually his life made a dramatic turn. Lewis emerged during the World War II years as a religious broadcaster who became famous as "the apostle to skeptics," in Britain and abroad, especially in the United States. His wartime radio essays defending and explaining the Christian faith comforted the fearful and wounded, and were eventually collected and published in America, as *Mere Christianity*, in 1952.

There has been no shortage of detractors and haters of the Bible down through the generations. But the Father, Himself has miraculously protected and preserved it so that we might be able to fully, and unequivocally trust it!

CONTRADICTIONS IN THE BIBLE
—NOT A CHANCE!

"Will unbelievers make the faithfulness of God of no effect?
Certainly not! Indeed, let God be true but every man a liar."
—Paul the Apostle

Detractors of the Bible often make the stinging criticism that it's a book full of contradictions. I couldn't disagree more! It's important if you're going to be a serious student of the Bible that you understand, first and foremost, that it can be believed. The Word of God has been preserved throughout the generations amidst many attempts to destroy it. It simply cannot be done! Most would agree that it has been protected by God, Himself. I concur. "The grass withers, the flower fades, but the Word of God stands forever." The end result can be serious; The obvious danger of these Bible detractors is, if we're not careful, the words they use can cause us to be skeptical of what we read. It can shake our confidence in the Word, which ultimately leads to doubt and then full-blown unbelief! It's very important that we exercise our faith to believe that the Word of God is first, and above all "inspired" by God, and secondly that it's inerrant in its scope.

But what about the verses that seem to contradict other verses? That's a fair question. The Bible says about God that He cannot lie. Therefore, He cannot and would not even if He could contradict Himself. So, how do we process those verses that appear problematic as it relates to contradictions?

Anytime you happen onto a verse that looks like a contradiction, the problem is not with what the Word says, but in your understanding of what it says. The more we read, study and meditate on God's Word the broader our understanding becomes. What we couldn't encompass awhile back has a way of coming into clearer view as we remain steadfast in our journey. The things that appear as contradictions, and there are more than a few, require more inspection, more meditation, and prayer. And, sometimes it's just a matter of letting those verse(s) marinate in your spirit until they clear up. There's no doubt about it, these things always require more effort, but you'll find that the extra effort is well worth your time.

The payoff in dealing with contradictory verses is that once we apply ourselves to get to the bottom of the truth, we have so much more to offer the rest of the world in terms of simplifying the Scriptures. You'll be able to help others navigate the minefield of what many would call, outright contradictions.

So, don't get all twisted up when you see or hear of contradictions in the Bible.

There's not a chance!

ENGAGE:

More than a few times Paul emphatically teaches that we are justified by faith, and not by works. (Rom. 3:28; 5:1; Gal. 2:16; 3:24). But James writes in his letter, "You see then that a man is justified by works, and not by faith only." (Jas 2:24) As you can clearly see, this appears to be an outright contradiction. But, remember what you learned above; The problem is not with what the Word says, but with our understanding of the Word. A closer examination of what the two apostles were stating begins to get clearer. Paul says we're justified by faith. But, in James' letter, he declares that "faith without works is dead"! If you think about it, they're both saying the same thing! A genuine and authentic faith always produces good works! So, you see, it isn't a contradiction at all but a clarification of the truth!

Learn to look closer when you are dealing with what appears to be a contradiction.

YOU CAN UNDERSTAND THE BIBLE!

"The Bible is not a difficult book to understand. It was written by men of common sense and by the application of common sense to its teachings, you will understand most of it, if not all of it."

—Billy Sunday

We are living in the information age. With the advent of digital technology, personal computers, the Internet and sites such as *Wikipedia* and *Google* information about anything is literally right at your fingertips! You can log onto hundreds of sites such as these mentioned and get thousands of articles and bits of information about any topic you desire in a matter of seconds.

If you think about all this from God's standpoint, it just doesn't make sense that the Bible would be un-understandable (misunderstood) for common people like us. I say that not to speak down to you but as a compliment! In Jesus's day, the Jewish people, the Scribes and the Pharisees couldn't understand what Jesus was saying, mainly because it didn't fit into their legalistic paradigm. But, a little hidden, obscure part of a verse says a very lot to me in thinking about this. "And the common people gladly heard Him." (Mt. 12:37) It was an amazing phenomenon. The much more refined Jews prided themselves in their knowledge of the Law and spiritual matters. But they just couldn't seem to understand the simple, yet profound, things that Jesus taught. "But the common people gladly "heard" Him!"

I think there are times and places for teaching the deeper things of the Bible. I enjoy doing that myself. But for most of my Sunday messages from the pulpit and especially for the purposes for this book, simple is better. My goal as a pastor/teacher/leader is not to impress people with what I know but to teach like Jesus taught. He taught in such a way that anyone, even those who had no spiritual orientation whatsoever, couldn't miss the truths contained in what He said! That's my goal!

Case in point: Jesus said, "I am the vine, you are the branches. He who abides in Me, and I in him, bears much fruit; for without Me you can do nothing." (Jn 15:5). It's obvious that you don't have to be a rocket scientist to understand what Jesus is saying here. It's the case with just about everything He said; not complicated, not stated in such a way as only the scholarly could understand but stated in a way you couldn't miss the Truth!

As you continue through this book, there will be many more easy to understand tips you'll be able to apply to simplify and to help you enjoy your Bible reading.

So, yes, you can understand the Bible!

WHEN YOU DON'T UNDERSTAND IT, DON'T SWEAT IT!

"In the Word of God, there is sweet and wholesome nourishment, milk for babies, honey for those that are grown up."

—Matthew Henry

In your reading/study time with your Bible, you're going to happen on to lots of things you don't understand. Don't worry about that. As you become more familiar with the Word and as you grow in maturity in your relationship with the Father many of those things will become crystal clear. I vividly remember early on in my walk with the Lord there were so many things I read that didn't make sense to me. But, over time, as I've continued to pursue the Truth, I have been able to get a grasp on those things that were confusing to me at the time.

It's also a good rule of thumb, even with the words and verses that you think you thoroughly understand that you give them another look and some further consideration from time to time. It's common for the Holy Spirit to give you a deeper understanding of things when you allow Him to do that. It almost seems like there are "layers" of truth in the Bible. It's truly an amazing Book! There will be some things you read that you immediately feel like you have a handle on, even if you happen to be a novice in your understanding. And, then maybe years later, you read that same verse, and you receive much greater insight. You see things that you couldn't see before. As long as you set your heart to be a "learner," you'll likely experience this phenomenon from now on.

So, relax. Don't get too "uptight" when you read something that you don't understand. Keep moving, keep reading and by all means keep listening to the Holy Spirit as He guides you into all truth.

SECTION 4

BIBLE VERSIONS:
WHICH ONE SHOULD I CHOOSE?

"All truth passes through three stages. First, it is ridiculed. Second, it is violently opposed. Third, it is accepted as being self-evident."

—Arthur Schopenhauer

It's a good question and one that most people wrestle with at least once in their life. There's a lot of Bible versions out there. I wouldn't discourage you in buying, or reading, any of them, but I do have my own preferences. I say "preferences" for a reason. I started with a *New King James Version* (Open Bible*) nearly thirty-five years ago, and that's the exact version I still use today. I like it for several reasons. For starters, it reads much easier than the *King James Version*. It excludes the language of 16th century English. For me, the *King James* is just hard to read. It's cumbersome, stiff and the language bogs me down. But I do use the *King James* very often in my study because the *Strong's Concordance* is "keyed," and numbered to it. So, I'll look at it often to help clarify what I'm reading and studying. *The New King James* keeps the integrity of the original text but is much easier to understand. A lot of people use the New American Standard or the New International Version. I like how they read and refer to them from time to time as well, but I cut my teeth, so to speak, on the NKJV and still love it today.

Many people are hardcore KJV when in all actuality it is just another version of the Bible. No one has a copy of the "original text." I've seen quite a few churches in the South, such as Alabama, Florida, Georgia and North Carolina who even state emphatically on their church sign, "King James Only." I would guess they might classify you as a heretic if you used any other version of the Bible. But, I think that's way more rigid than it should be. Most people do have a genuine reverence for the *King James Version*, and with good reason, because for many, it was the first Bible they read. It is both respectable and reliable. But, new readers of the Bible are prone to put it down due to the stiffness of the language. My advice is not to stop there but to find one that's easy for you to read and that maintains historical integrity. To each his own.

There are also more than a few out there that are considered "transliterations." A transliteration is what I'd call a "loose" translation

There's *The Living Bible*, *The New Living Translation*, *Good News for Modern Man*, and my favorite, Eugene Peterson's, *The Message*. All these (there are others) have become quite popular with many people mainly because they are so easily read. The very first Bible that I started reading was a little paperback *The Living Bible*. I found it easy to read, easy to understand. In fact, I read it faithfully until I got to the book of Leviticus and encountered all those "begats." I didn't understand it, got bogged down there, and put the Bible down for several years. My point is this: if you find a version that's easy for you to read, read on! You can always change to another version somewhere down the road.

I do think it's important to stay close to the KJV even if it's just for deeper study purposes only. But, there's no doubt about it, the Lord will bless your reading whatever version you choose to read. If your heart is open, and you're genuinely looking for truth, He will continue to lead you in the right direction.

ENGAGE:

Do some research into several different translations of the Bible. If you are Internet, or even smartphone, proficient this will be very easy for you to do. (*YouVersion* is a great Bible app for smartphones. I use it often and find it to be very helpful).

Do some reading from different Bibles and see how they "feel" to you. You can do this before you make any investment in a nice Bible. If you're a churchgoer, it would also make sense to find out what translation of the Bible your pastor uses to make it easier for you to follow along.

The Bible I started with was a NKJV version of *The Open Bible* (Thomas Nelson Publishing, Nashville, TN). I highly recommend this study Bible because of the additional resources included within.

In *The Open Bible* at the beginning of each book, you are given a paragraph, and brief description, that's simple and easy to understand:

Example: **The Book of John**
- The Book of John
- The Author of John

- The Time of John
- The Christ of John
- Keys to John
- Key Verses/Key Chapters in the Book of John
- Survey of John
- A graphic showing the significant points of the book
- Footnotes: crossreferences; further explanations, etc
- Graphics and stories within each chapter to illustrate a certain principle, person or place.
- An extensive outline of the entire book

These things have been extremely helpful to me in learning to study the Bible.

COMMENTARIES:
WELL, OK, BUT BE CAREFUL!

"We must compare the words of Christ in Scripture to the teachings of any man, and if the man contradicts Christ, he understands nothing."

—Jeff Baldwin

It's customary as people begin to get serious about studying the Bible to use the assistance of the many available commentaries. I think that can be a very good thing, to a degree. For instance, I have in my computer Bible programs at least a dozen or more commentaries that I peruse from time to time. Many times I'll go to one or more of those resources to get another perspective on something I'm reading, studying or preparing to teach. More often than not I'll compare several of those commentaries. There are times I'll read things that confirm what I was already thinking and other times I'll get an entirely different viewpoint, which can also be very helpful.

The important thing to remember when using a commentary is to understand that you are drawing from another person's knowledge, experience, wisdom, and spiritual orientation. That has the potential to bring you into a greater understanding of your area of study. But, I would caution you in your use of commentaries in that you are always receiving from writers who have a unique, and sometimes controversial, (and possibly erroneous) slant on Scripture. That's not always bad, but it has the potential to lead novice readers into error. For instance, if you're reading from a commentary of someone who is a staunch legalist you're going to come away with a very legalistic viewpoint. If you "buy into" every single thing they write you're going to find yourself becoming legalistic, as well. That can be a slippery slope if you're not careful. Some Bible commentaries deny the validity of the gifts of the Holy Spirit, saying they are not relevant for today. Others may deny the reality of the supernatural realm altogether, teaching that God is not in the miracle business anymore. There are yet other commentators who are prisoners to denominational bias and theological mindset. So, you can clearly see my point.

Matthew Henry's Commentary, a popular commentary which was written several centuries ago, goes into great detail on every single verse.

It's a little harder to read, but it can give you a lot to consider. I use it fairly often, and I think it helps to broaden my thinking on a subject. But, I do from time to time find myself disagreeing with some of his points. The commentaries I like the best are the ones that don't give a lot of personal opinions but define the Hebrew and Greek words in today's meanings. Those are the ones that can really deepen your understanding without hazing you into the ditch in any direction.

Commentaries are OK. Use them at your discretion. But, understand, it's still the best route to read, pray, dig, investigate, meditate, compare other verses, maybe even other Bible versions, and get in a position to listen to the leading and prompting of the Holy Spirit. He is, after all, our Teacher. We are promised that He will lead us into all Truth. The Father wants you to have a good handle on what the Word is saying, and there's not a commentary out there that can come close to the Holy Spirit! You can't go wrong there! You'll learn to draw your conclusions from the things He shows you. He's determined to help! That's a guarantee!

BIOGRAPHICAL STUDIES

"The Bible is full of examples of people who dreamed big, and God Blessed them."

—Tracie Peterson

Character Study

A character study is the study of a particular Bible person to find their habits, inclinations, character traits, personality traits, perspectives, achievements, and even failures. A character study can give one much deeper insight into their lives and how they fit in the entire scheme of the Bible.

I really enjoy doing character studies as it has a way of helping me to understand many of the very interesting people in the Bible. For instance, a study on Peter would reveal a man that was extremely rambunctious in nature. When Jesus was walking on the water He said, "Come," and Peter got out of the boat and onto the water. When the soldiers came to seize Jesus in the garden, it was Peter who drew his sword and cut the ear off one of the soldiers. You would find that it was also this same man that told Jesus, "they may all (the other disciples) forsake you, but I won't." He meant it, but he had no idea the extent of the frailty of his own flesh. And, you may know the story, after the rooster crowed he had denied Jesus three times! He was the same man that, after Jesus' resurrection, Jesus asked the daunting question, "Do you love me?" Peter had failed Jesus at a time when he desperately needed him. His failure was obviously greater than any failure you will ever experience. It would have been easy for Peter to let that failure define the rest of his life. It happens to people all the time. But God had a greater plan for Peter, and something deep and profound happened in Peter the night Jesus posed that question, "Do you love me?" those three times. The reason I know something happened is because for the next 20-25 years Peter was the most important man on the planet as it related to the advancement of the kingdom of God. His encounter with Jesus after His resurrection made all the difference! It'll do the same for you! When I'm reading 1 and 2 Peter, I take all those things into consideration, and it helps me to get a much better handle on everything Peter wrote.

There is an almost unlimited number of Bible characters that you could study. Those kind of things can deeply enhance your Bible reading.

If you decide to roll up your sleeves and do studies on Bible characters, you'll find many details on some remarkable people! It'll make your Bible reading much more productive and enjoyable.

ENGAGE:

Paul would be a great, and very interesting, person on which to do biographical study. There is an unlimited amount of evidence of his life before, and after, Christ! Add to that the letters that he penned and the content represented there you will come to many conclusions about this incredible servant of the Lord. As you read his letters and begin to understand the magnitude of trials, tests, near death experiences and such, you'll appreciate what he has written to a much greater degree!

- Where do you see Paul (Saul) first mentioned?
- What was his mission at that time?
- What happened to Paul to change the course of his life?
- What characteristics did his conversion produce?
- What personality traits do you notice?
- How did he receive his training?
- When/how did he first come onto the scene as a leader/apostle?
- What were the challenges he was faced with?
- How deep was his commitment to the call on his life?
- How did Paul finish "his race?"

These and dozens of other questions you might devise will help you immensely as you conduct this biographical study. Enjoy!

BOOK STUDIES

"The Bible has been one of the greatest motivators of those who believe its content."

—Elmer Towns

Book Studies

A book study is the in-depth study of a particular book, or letter, of the Bible. The study of a book or a letter in the Bible is another great way to deepen your understanding and make your Bible reading more enjoyable. When planning to do a book study one should take into consideration things such as:

1) Who wrote the book?
2) What was the time of the writing?
3) What were the customs during that time?
4) Where was the book written? (for instance, Paul was in prison when he wrote some of his writings)
5) To whom was the book written?
6) What is this book's main purpose?
7) How does this book compare with other things the writer has written?
8) How does this book compare with what others have written?
9) What are the spiritual principles that the writer is trying to establish?
10) What were the challenges presented to the truth being accepted during that time?

There may be more to add to that list, but you get the idea.

One thing to remember when studying a letter is to simply remind yourself that it is a letter. You may already know this, but the chapter numbers and verse numbers were added to help us in our Bible reading. A lot of the time they do help, but not always. I would, just for the fun of it, read part, or all, of one of Paul's letters without stopping at the end of a chapter. Just read it straight through occasionally, and you'll be reading it just the way he wrote it!

In summation, the study of a certain book calls for you to thoroughly investigate the writing as much as you can. You can compare this with character, or biographical, studies to get great insight into a book or letter and the person who penned it.

WORD STUDIES

"Learning never exhausts the mind."

—Leonardo da Vinci

A Bible word study is the practice of identifying, tracking and researching a particular word in Scripture.

Learning to do Biblical word studies can be a very rewarding and fulfilling exercise in your journey to study the Bible. Very often discovering the true meaning of a single word, and understanding it in the context of Scripture, can open up a much broader view and give light and greater meaning to the entire verse. Occasionally that one word will make all the difference in the clarity, and truth of the verse. Remember, most of what we are reading today is a derivative from the original *King James Version* and the language and word meanings from the 1600s. The meaning of a word in 1600 might have an altogether different meaning for us today.

It's important to remember when beginning a word study that the Old Testament was translated from the Hebrew language and the New Testament was translated from the Greek. In starting the study of a single word, it's important to find the very first usage of that word in the Bible. You can do this with your *Strong's Concordance.* Then you can begin to follow the word and how it's used through the whole Bible

Strong's will give you the definition, but you'll get a much better handle on the meaning of the word as you read and see how it's used within different contexts in other places in your Bible. Make some notes along the way and draw some conclusions as you compare how the word is used. Pay particular attention to the context in which the word is used. Remember, you're trying to get to the root meaning of the word you're studying.

There is so much user-friendly Bible software (and free, online tools) out there that has made the exercise of doing word studies much easier. If you're interested in speed and accuracy, then I recommend you use some of those. But, if you don't have access to a computer you can still do word studies the old fashioned way. Either way, word studies will increase your knowledge and enrich your understanding as you study your Bible.

ENGAGE:

This should be a fun word study for you, and it'll open your eyes to what you might discover when you start to look closer at what is written in the Word.

I have asked this question several times to our church throughout the years, always telling them that it's a trick question. Without fail, 90% of them will fall for the same question every time. The question I ask is, "How many of you have read about the antichrist in the book of Revelation?" I won't give it away, but I think you'll be surprised by what you discover.

- Use the Strong's Concordance to look up the word, "antichrist."
- What is the definition?
- How many times is it used?
- Where (what books) is it used?
- How is it used?
- What Biblical author(s) used the word?
- What are your conclusions?

This is a productive exercise to spark your interest in doing word studies. You'll find them with just a little extra effort you'll uncover some very profound truths!

THE HEBREW AND GREEK

"Study to shew thyself approved unto God, a workman that needs not to be ashamed, rightly dividing the word of truth."
—Paul the Apostle

One of the things that can revolutionize your reading and study of the Bible is to begin to consider the Hebrew and Greek languages, the original languages that our current Bible was translated from. Just the thought of trying to learn another language can be downright intimidating, but I'd like to encourage you not to go there. I thought the same thing years ago. Now, I don't have a seminary education. If I had, I would have been exposed to the original languages much earlier. Courses on both the Hebrew and Greek languages are part of the common curriculum of most Bible colleges, as they should be.

For the first few years of my "new life" in the Lord, I steered away from the Hebrew and Greek believing that I would never need that as part of my learning, and study of the Bible. As I matured, I began hearing friends that I trusted talk about certain Hebrew and Greek words. It sparked my curiosity, so I cautiously proceeded forward. On advice from someone who I considered a "big brother" in the Lord I bought that big, intimidating, scary looking book called the *Strong's Concordance*. It's about 4 inches thick, weighs a few pounds and looks a lot like the first dictionary I remember seeing. Intimidating to look at, to say the least. But, I found out that it's not an intimidating book at all. Much to the contrary. It's very easy to use, and with a little help and practice, you'll have it mastered in no time at all. It could very well revolutionize your overall Bible study and your understanding of keywords and how they're used.

The *Strong's Concordance* is, simply, a dictionary and is a very useful tool for studying the scriptures. It takes every single word of the *King James Version* and lists where each word can be found in the scriptures. It is useful for locating scripture verses that you know the words to, but don't know the book, chapter, and verse. Also beside each verse reference, there is a number. That number represents a Hebrew word (Old Testament) or Greek word (New Testament). In the back of the book, it lists Hebrew and Greek words used to translate the Bible into English and gives their definition. It also lets the reader directly compare how the same word may be used elsewhere in the Bible.

There are now so many online resources that you can gain a workable understanding of the Hebrew and Greek language without spending a dime. In fact, I would advise against buying the big, bulky Strong's altogether. If you are computer or smartphone literate, you can easily look up Greek and Hebrew words and their definitions without any problem. Other resources I have found extremely helpful are:

The Interlinear Bible
I really like this one, and I find myself using it a lot! I have it in my computer Bible programs. I also discovered in the process of preparing for this book that Billy Graham was a devout user of the Interlinear Bible. This is the ONLY Bible that includes the complete Hebrew and Greek texts with a direct English translation below each word. It also includes "The Literal Translation of the Bible" so you can easily read through the Bible, learning keywords as you go. Strong's numbers are printed directly above the Hebrew and Greek words, so you don't need prior knowledge of Greek or Hebrew to dig even deeper into Scripture and its meaning. Again, I wouldn't buy the book but use the online version instead.

Theological Wordbook of the Old/New Testament
A good number of trusted Bible scholars have written articles on many of the important, and keywords in both the Old and New Testaments. This work is also "keyed" to the *Strong's Concordance*.

Vine's Bible Dictionary
This timeless classic is THE reference guide to both Old and New Testament Hebrew and Greek words for English readers. It explains the meaning of the original Greek with the added dimension of the context of the Greek word. It was produced especially for the help of those who do not routinely study Hebrew or Greek. All entries in both OT and NT dictionaries are organized alphabetically in English, along with the Hebrew or Greek words from which they are translated.

These I have listed are my favorites but there are a lot of other resources out there that you might find helpful and more often than not you can find them online for FREE!

You don't have to have an understanding of the Hebrew and Greek, but it will definitely broaden your understanding of many important Biblical words. I think it is important!

I encourage you to explore both the Hebrew and Greek. I promise you'll be glad you did!

THE *LOGOS* AND THE *RHEMA*

"The Word is the face, the countenance, the representation of God, in whom He is brought to light and made known."
—Claudius of Alexandria

These are two important Greek words that demand a definition for any serious student of the Bible. Both *logos* and *rhema* are translated into English in your Bible as, "word." And while that seems simple enough, they each have a different meaning. A distinction can be made between the two by looking at how they're used in the context of Scripture. While the definitions may be broader than I'll cover here a simple definition is as follows:

In the beginning was the Word (Logos), and the Word was with God, and the Word was God.

John 1:1

As you probably know by now, the above verse is not talking about the Bible but about Jesus, Himself. The Greek word, *logos*, is a word used to describe Jesus as the Word becoming flesh, or even better yet, the "Living Word"; the person of revelation or the whole deity in whom the Father becomes known. The Greek understanding of the universe includes *logos* as the wisdom and designer that holds it together. Great Greek philosophers like Aristotle and Plato use the term *logos* to describe "the all-powerful, all-knowing God."

Man shall not live by bread alone, but by every word (rhema) that proceeds out of the mouth of God.

Luke 4:4

Jesus responds to Satan using specific words to rebuke him. In this passage it's like the "sword of the Spirit" Paul refers to in Ephesians 6:17. The Greek word, *rhema* is used 70 times to indicate a word that is spoken by God, specifically to a person or group. So, when you look at the above verse, it makes it much clearer to know the definition: "Man shall not live by bread alone but by every *rhema*, or specific word spoken to them by God." One must make the obvious conclusion that the *rhema* word is not just limited to the Bible and the specific things that God spoke to different ones, but the reality that He also speaks the *rhema* (personal, specific) word to us today, as well.

Here's an example of a personal *rhema* word God spoke to my spirit in that "still, small voice" some ten years ago, "Andy, there's a shift in how this works; normally people move to an area because of a job, and then they find a church. I'm changing that. I'm going to bring people in here from all over, and I will give them a job." You can imagine the ramifications of that personal, *rhema*, word from the Father. It might even seem far-fetched to you. But, the Father loves speaking those things to our spirit to ignite our faith. As a church we started to declare that and pray consistently about it, and it began to happen. Last count, over 250 or more had moved here as a result of that "*rhema*" word from the Lord. And, after ten years it is still happening!

HERMENEUTICS AND HOMILETICS

"Let us, therefore, yield ourselves and bow to the authority of the
Holy Scriptures, which can neither err nor deceive."

—Augustine of Hippo

I was thirty years old before I went to church in any regular manner.
Up to that time in my life, I had probably only been in a church, counting
funerals and weddings, less than 20 times. I only say that so you can
understand how far I was behind the curve of knowing anything about
the Bible. I believed in God; I believed the Word was true even though
I knew absolutely nothing about it. I did go to Vacation Bible School a
few times and, there, heard the stories of David and Goliath, Shadrach,
Meshach and Abed-Nego and other Bible heroes. But as far as being able
to pick up a Bible and know where or how to read, or find anything, I was
completely lost.

When I started my growth, learning, and understanding at age 30,
I was like a sponge. I had a strong hunger for the Word and the things
of the Lord. I couldn't get enough of it, and I applied myself to learn.
I'm happy to say that after all these years I'm still hungry and still in the
process of learning from the Bible.

Somewhere along the way, I started hearing new words that other
people seemed to know the meaning of but I had no idea what they
were talking about. I think, if we're not careful, we can let ourselves get
intimidated by those words and shrink back away from them and never
really understand what they mean. That was my position at one time.

These two words, hermeneutics, and homiletics are two that were
intimidating to me. I went a few years and avoided finding what they were
about. What I found out when I did start to look is these are words that
shouldn't be intimidating at all. A clear understanding of them will help
you as you pursue the Truth. So, for the purpose of this chapter, I want to
define these two words so as to demystify them.

Hermeneutics is the theory and methodology of Biblical interpretation.
Hermeneutics was initially applied to the "interpretation, or exegesis," of
scripture. The terms "hermeneutics" and "exegesis" are sometimes used
interchangeably. Hermeneutic refers to a particular method of interpretation.

Homiletics is the art of preaching. Homiletics comprises the study
and delivery of a sermon or other religious discourse and involves all
forms of preaching.

EXEGESIS OR EISEGESIS?
BE CAREFUL WHEN MAKING
THAT CHOICE!

"There are only two ways you can study the Bible; Studying it with your mind made up; Studying it to let it make up your mind."

—Author Unknown

Exegesis, eisegesis … what do those words even mean? I had seen them a few times, and they meant absolutely nothing to me. But, as it turns out, they're both extremely important words in terms of Bible study. How you understand and, what you do with these two words in practice will largely determine whether or not you'll be able to be trusted in communicating the things you learn in the Bible.

Exegesis is the interpretation of a text, or passage of Scripture, through a thorough analysis of its content in order to clarify its meaning. Our main task in exegesis is to discover the original, intended meaning of a given text through careful, systematic study. It's the process of examining a text to discern what its first readers would have understood it to mean.

Eisegesis, on the other hand, is best understood when contrasted with exegesis. While exegesis is the process of drawing out the meaning from a text in accordance with the context and discoverable meaning of its author, eisegesis occurs when a reader imposes his or her interpretation into and onto the text.

As you can see, there is a difference in those two words. It might even appear to be just a subtle difference at first glance, but the ramifications in consistent practice of eisegesis are apt to bring about some enormous, and oftentimes completely erroneous, results.

It's very common for someone studying the Bible to make this deadly mistake. After all, we want to prove our point. So, we set out to find the evidence to back up or support our little theory, our mindset or our foregone conclusions. We can nearly always find the evidence we need. And, voila, we prove to ourselves, and sadly sometimes prove it to others as well, we're right again. This happens all the time, and it's a very dangerous practice; one that I would guess the Lord detests very much.

I love any kind of movie about lawyers, trials, the courtroom, etc. Always have. It's intriguing to me to see how a seasoned and crafty lawyer presents his evidence and argues his case before the jury. I was watching a documentary recently where a man was being tried for the murder of his wife. The prosecution alleged that he had pushed her down the second-floor flight of stairs to her death. Of course, the defense argument was that she had fallen. Volumes of evidence were presented over the course of the long trial. Both sides presented a very solid and convincing case. As it turned out the forensic expert acquired by the prosecution testified under oath certain details about the blood spatter, the DNA and the certainty that the blood evidence could not have possibly been compromised, or tampered with. It was revealed later that the expert had lied. Whether or not the lead prosecutor was privy to that lie was not determined. But, what did stand out that shed a negative light on the entire prosecution team was that they set out at the very beginning to try to prove their point, even to the degree of ignoring extremely important evidence. The lying forensic expert jeopardized the entire case of the prosecution, and the man was awarded a new trial. It was more important to them to win the case, even if they had to cheat a little than actually to see truth and justice prevail. That happens all the time in the courtroom, but it shouldn't happen in our study, and interpretation of the Bible.

It's much the same with the eisegesis crowd. It seems that they'd rather be right than to see Truth and justice prevail, as well. Just like in the courtroom, the evidence speaks. It's the difference in reading, studying, examining the Word and letting the evidence we uncover lead us to our conclusions, and ultimately our convictions, rather than having a preconceived idea, or conclusion, or some little pet doctrine and digging for evidence to prove our point.

A. *Exegesis* leads to Truth, integrity and accurate Biblical interpretation. It is objective, analytical, researched, and referenced, etc.

B. *Eisegesis* is subjective, non-analytical, and from a personal bias.

Make sure you don't find yourself in the big crowd that's trying just a little too hard to prove their point.

ITALICIZED WORDS

"Isn't it amazing that almost everyone has an opinion to offer about the Bible, and yet so few have studied it?"

—R.C. Sproul

In the process of your Bible reading, you'll often come across words that are italicized. When you see that you'll know that these are words that were not in the original text. They are words that have been added to make it easier and smoother for you to read and in some cases make what has been written clearer and easier to understand. I think in most cases these added words are helpful, but not always.

There could be hundreds of examples, but one that helps to make this point is found in 1 Corinthians 12:1. This chapter is such an important, and pivotal, one as it relates to the gifts of the Spirit that it doesn't need to be misinterpreted or misunderstood. "Now concerning spiritual gifts, brethren, I do not want you to be ignorant." If you'll notice in your Bible the word, "gifts," there is italicized which, again means it was not in the original text. The actual Greek word there is, "*pneumatikos*" which simply means, "things of the Spirit." I don't think italicizing the word, "gifts," is a dangerous misinterpretation at all but I do think we should take a closer look and see what it says without that word and let the Spirit lead us deeper in our understanding.

Another good example is found in Romans 12:9. *The New King James Version* reads this way, "Let love be without hypocrisy. Abhor what is evil. Cling to what is good." Some simple, yet profound, advice to say the least. But when you look closer at the italicized words, you'll find that "Let," and "be" are both italicized. In this instance, at least for me, it changes the thrust of what Paul is writing to the Romans. Instead of reading, "Let love be without hypocrisy," it would actually say, "Love without hypocrisy." Paul's not laying down a doctrinal declaration nor is he issuing a Biblical commandment. But, what he is doing here (when you remove those two words) is communicating in a very straightforward, and powerful, way the encouragement to "love, and to do it genuinely!" Another way of looking at it would be that Paul's not saying, "when" you love, do it without hypocrisy, but simply, he's saying, just do it! Without hypocrisy! Be a lover! And, don't be hypocritical in the process!

I heard a preacher one time preach an entire message over a word that was italicized. I don't think he even knew it! If clear, correct Bible interpretation is important, and we know that it is, I think that's an area where one should be extremely cautious. We should also be extremely careful not to try and build doctrine around words that are not in the original text!!

Sometimes it just helps to read the text skipping over the italicized words. Occasionally you'll find that it can change, albeit many times ever so minutely, the actual meaning of the verse.

Start to look for those italicized words, and it'll help you to be a much better student of the Bible.

SECTION 5

WHICH COVENANT, OLD, OR NEW?

"This cup is the new covenant in My blood, which is shed for you."

—Jesus

It's extremely important when studying your Bible to understand which covenant is in effect. While there are a number of different covenants throughout the Bible, I'll limit this chapter in explaining the "main two." Your Bible is divided into two main sections, the Old Testament, or Old Covenant and the New Testament, or New Covenant. The Old Covenant is a covenant of Law, more specifically the Jewish Law while the New Covenant is a Covenant of grace. There's a vast difference between law and grace and an equally vast difference between Old and New Covenant.

One of the clearest examples is to look at the life of the apostle Paul. When we first see him in Scripture, he is an extremely staunch proponent of the Jewish Law. Staunch enough as it was, his chief aim in life was to see those who proclaimed Jesus and the resurrection brought before the courts, judged to be guilty and then see them stoned to death. It's believed that he was the instigator when Stephen was put to death in that very manner. At the very least he was a willing, and agreeing participant. But, soon after Paul had an encounter with Jesus on the road and it changed everything. He was stricken with blindness for a time but came out of that time with greater vision, so to speak, about spiritual things. He began to learn about Jesus, the resurrection and the New Covenant that Jesus ushered in with His death, burial and resurrection. It was as dramatic of a 180-degree turn as has ever happened in history! One day he was seeking to destroy these Jesus followers, and literally the next day he was one of them, himself.

In the first century, there was not a more qualified person on the planet to talk about grace and to contrast that vast difference between law and grace, than Paul. That is due, largely in part, to the fact that he knew the Jewish law inside and out but, now, after being exposed to grace, he saw everything completely different. That encounter totally transformed his thinking away from "rules" oriented religion to one centered around a personal relationship with the Father. Paul had a stubborn determination up until the time of his own death to communicate grace to anyone who would listen. He was determined never to be a part of anyone being caught up in the same dead religion, and its rules and practices, that he had been a prisoner of. It cost him everything; his friends, his Jewish counterparts, his reputation as a Pharisee; it even almost cost him his life more than a few times. But, in the end, Paul said it was worth it all to have "gained" Christ!

Yet indeed I also count all things loss for the excellence of the knowledge of Christ Jesus my Lord, for whom I have suffered the loss of all things, and count them as rubbish, that I may gain Christ.

Phil 3:8-9

You will notice that Paul starts, and finishes, every single one of his letters mentioning grace. I call those quotes the "bookends" of each of his letters. It doesn't matter what topic Paul is addressing in the body of his letters; they are encased, communicated and taught within the context of grace! Everything Paul did and said from the time of his encounter with Jesus was done from the standpoint of grace and his deepening and ongoing understanding of the New Covenant and his relationship with the Father.

This chapter is extremely important to get a grasp on as you learn to see the difference in law and grace and the distinction between what is Old Covenant, and what is New Covenant.

Those not making the distinction between the Old Covenant and the New Covenant can easily develop thought patterns, and then mindsets, that are not consistent with where the Lord wants to take us. For instance, a couple of very obvious examples would be; The Law states, "an eye for and eye, and a tooth for a tooth." One reading that could quickly ascertain that when we are offended, wounded or even physically injured by someone that we have Biblical permission to retaliate. That might be so under the Old Covenant, but that kind of thinking and behavior is far from the revolutionary principles that Jesus taught under the New Covenant.

Whoever slaps you on your right cheek, turn the other to him also.

Matt 5:39

Another obvious example lies in Deuteronomy 21, under the Levitical law if a man had a rebellious son he should take him to the elders at the gates of the city and, there, stone him to death. Seems a little extreme to me but that's the way it was!

Another great example is when you look at the New Covenant you see Jesus's story about the prodigal son. The dad in the story, who is clearly a type of the Father, had a rebellious son who took his inheritance, left the farm and blew all his resources by careless, and loose living. Upon returning, the father in the story saw him a long way off, ran to him, fell on his neck, had compassion on him, kissed him and welcomed him home. There you can plainly see the vast difference between the Old Covenant and the New Covenant.

It's extremely important when reading your Bible that you understand that you are not under the "Law," now, but under grace! Understand the covenants, and you'll understand the Bible much better!

WHERE DO I START?

"Just do it!"

—Nike

I hear this question often, and it's a legitimate one—one that requires an adequate, calculated and specific answer. For novice Bible readers, knowing where to start is probably the most important thing to consider after you've made the brilliant decision to read the Bible in the first place. I hear a variation of this explanation very often, "I just flip through the pages and stick my finger in, and that's where I start reading. That's where God wants to speak to me." And, believe me, I don't doubt one bit that God can and will speak to you from the Word if that's your method. In fact, I believe He'll take any opportunity He gets with you to get and keep, you interested in what the Word says. But, let's think about it in a more mature and strategic fashion.

When I started reading that little paperback Living Bible in my twenties, I didn't know any different than to just start on page one. I mean that's how you start reading any book. And, while I can honestly say that I learned and grew from reading from the start, I wouldn't at all instruct anyone to start at the first of the Bible now. I now know there's a much better method. I've heard many Bible teachers give the advice to start reading in the gospel of John. I think that's great advice. If not John I would advise starting with one of the other three writers of the gospels, Matthew, Mark or Luke. They each have their different literary styles, their unique attitudes, and perspectives of what, and how, they saw and interpreted Jesus's every move. But, the key point here is that each of them had been with Jesus; they knew Him! Their perspective was a personal one, and they tell their story, firsthand. It makes sense if you think about it; if you're going to read a story about anyone, the ones who knew the person, and in this case lived with Jesus day in and day out, would definitely be the ones you wanted to read. They would know more about the person than someone who didn't have that personal experience. So yes, start with Matthew, Mark, Luke or John.

Another key reason for starting in the gospels is that you're starting with the story of Jesus! It's in the gospel that He begins teaching, explaining and establishing His kingdom. That's extremely important in understanding the Bible, overall. His kingdom was vastly different than the ritualistic practice of religion of the Jews in His time. His kingdom

121

was one marked by inclusion, grace, and love. When you begin your Bible reading experience, it's vital that you start to see the entire Scriptures through the lens of grace. It will make all the difference for you!

Somewhere along the way, you might want to incorporate reading the Psalms or Proverbs. I like doing that even today. And, it's interesting that there are thirty-one proverbs—one for each day of the month. You'll find that they're loaded with little practical bits of advice. They're easy to read, and you'll learn lots as you read them.

For others who have developed in maturity in their Bible reading, you can get even more strategic. Invest some time in learning about the different books of the Bible. Here are some things that will help. Who wrote the book/letter? What are the main themes of the book? What are the cultural conditions of the times? What ideas are the authors attempting to communicate? What are the spiritual principles being taught? What are the obstacles presented to the move of God and the assimilation of the "good news?"

As you mature into a more seasoned student of the Bible, there'll be times that you know the Father is directing you to a certain book or letter. By all means, go there! Other times the Holy Spirit will bring a verse, or maybe even a single word to your mind for you to look at more closely. When He does this, it's to give you a greater understanding of something that the Lord deems vital and relevant for you. When this happens, don't get in a hurry in your reading. Savor every word; think about it; meditate on it; cross-reference with other related verses; pray that the Holy Spirit will give you insight into it. You'll come out of those times with a much greater understanding of what is written in the Book.

These are some practical ways to help you in knowing where to start reading your Bible. It's important when reading your Bible that you read it with purpose. But, the most important advice can be taken from Nike's well-known tagline,: "Just Do It!"

THE PARABLES OF JESUS

"Jesus clearly gives parables to hide the meaning from those whose hearts are hardened."

—Unknown

Jesus was a teacher; But it's important to remember that He was not "just" a teacher but the greatest Teacher that has ever existed in either time or eternity, on Earth or elsewhere!! Everything about Jesus was/ is incredible. He is, after all, the Son of God! He had a unique way of teaching. Even though He possessed all wisdom and knew all things, He taught in such a way that literally anyone could understand His teachings. Those that had absolutely no spiritual orientation whatsoever could understand Jesus. There was an exception to that both in those days, and today. It's interesting to note that the only ones who had trouble understanding were those that were sure they had it all figured out. The Pharisees, Scribes and Sadducees, the religious crowd in Jesus's day could not understand His teaching, even as simple and understandable as it was! It seems to be a phenomenon that exists in our generation as well.

Jesus was a master storyteller. It's also interesting, and important to note, that people remember stories! They remember stories much easier than they remember Bible verses and content. Jesus stories were simple in nature but contained very deep, profound and life-changing truths! Many of the great Biblical truths came through clearly when He told His stories. Jesus told many of these stories through "parables." A parable is a simple story used to illustrate a moral or spiritual lesson. Parables both "conceal" a truth as well as "reveal" a truth. These parables are found almost exclusively in the gospels of Matthew (23), Mark (8) and Luke (24). John's gospel does use a few analogies, however, but those might or might not be considered to be parables in the strictest use of the term. At any rate, the parables were a major part of the teachings of Jesus.

Some say that a third of what Jesus taught was taught in parables. You will thoroughly enjoy reading them, and you'll grow from it. It will become clear that a simple story can accomplish great things in a person's life. Let's agree, there are times for teaching some of the deeper truths of the Bible. But, let's make our goal to be a teacher like Jesus and, rather than try to impress others with what we know, let's learn to teach in such a simple way that no one can miss the Truth contained!

ENGAGE:

There are seven parables in Matthew 13. Read them and identify the truths found therein.

PSALMS, PROVERBS, ECCLESIASTES, AND THE SONG OF SOLOMON

"The most valuable thing the Psalms do for me is to express that same delight in God which made David dance."

—C.S. Lewis

There are four books in the Bible that seem to be somewhat different than many of the other books. Psalms, Proverbs, Ecclesiastes and the Song of Solomon are ones that demand at least some definition.

PSALMS

Stick your thumb in the very center of your Bible, and you'll be right square in the middle of the book of Psalms. *Psalms* simply means songs and the psalms in the Bible were originally set to music. Many of those have even been successfully adapted to modern worship today. Although there are at least seven different writers of the Psalms David is the most prolific writer with at least 75 attributed to his authorship. There are others, somewhere around fifty, with which no author is named. When I think of the Psalms, I think of worship. And, while there are several different types of psalms including psalms of praise, prophetic psalms, psalms of thanksgiving, psalms of adoration of the Lord, even psalms of lament (a passionate expression of grief or sorrow), the entire book could easily be called a book of worship.

Many of the Psalms were penned during a 40 year stretch on the top of Mt Zion. There the Ark of the Covenant, which for generations had been behind the veil in the Most Holy Place, was now out in the open. And, for 40 years, non-stop, 24-7, night and day worship was going on. I can visualize David, laying his harp down, sitting down under the mercy wings on the Ark of the Covenant and starting to write; "The Lord is my Shepherd, I shall not want …." Then I picture him picking up his harp again and putting what he had written, to music. It must have been an incredible season to be alive.

You will enjoy reading the Psalms. As you read them, you'll get a great understanding from those who were experiencing the entire spectrum of valleys and victories, and how they communicated those things to the Father through worship.

PROVERBS

Immediately following Psalms in your Bible is the Book of Proverbs. The Book of Proverbs has been known as the "Book of Wisdom" from the very beginning. A proverb is simply, a "wise saying." Proverbs is packed with bite-sized bits of practical wisdom. It's written in such a way as to be very simple to understand, even to the most unlearned of readers. I still enjoy turning to Proverbs and reading the wisdom contained in them. Incidentally, there are thirty-one proverbs in number, one chapter for each day of the month! Many people read them that way, and some have consistently done that for years. Most Bible scholars give Solomon credit as being the author, although there are a few attributed to other writers.

ECCLESIASTES

Ecclesiastes is an interesting book of the Bible. It is written from the perspective of a King of Jerusalem as he relates his experiences and the lessons he has learned throughout his life. The author, traditionally believed to be Solomon, talks about the best way to live. The word, "vanity," is used more than thirty times in the Book of Ecclesiastes. The "Preacher," as the writer of the work defines himself, concludes that everything we do in life ends up in futile emptiness without God in our lives. Nothing can fill the God-shaped void in our lives but God, Himself! Everything else is a vain attempt at human contentment. The book concludes with this deduction: "Fear God, and keep his commandments; for that is the whole duty of everyone."

SONG OF SOLOMON

The Song of Solomon, sometimes also referred to as "The Song of Songs," is a love song written by Solomon as it depicts the courting and wedding of a "shepherdess" by King Solomon. Allegorically, it pictures Israel as God's betrothed bride and the church as the Bride of Christ. As human life finds its highest fulfillment in the love of man and woman, so spiritual life finds its highest fulfillment in the love of God for His people and Christ for His church. The book is arranged like scenes in a drama with three main speakers; the bride, the king, and the daughters of Jerusalem. The book reveals no reference, whatsoever, to the Law or to the Covenant but simply the voices of two lovers in harmony longing for one another.

THE BOOK OF REVELATION

"When studying the Book of Revelation remember, some of it has happened, some of it is happening, and some of it has yet to happen."

—Andy Taylor

The book of Revelation, the final book in the New Testament is an intriguing literary work. John, toward the end of his life and exiled to die as punishment on the volcanic island, Patmos, received this unfolding revelation which was given to him in several visions by the Lord. It begins with letters to the "Seven Churches of Asia." John then describes a series of prophetic visions including figures such as the Seven-Headed Dragon, The Serpent, and the Beast, culminating in the Second Coming of Jesus. This mysterious imagery has led to a wide variety of interpretations and has caused some argument and confusion by those attempting to interpret the book. While there is much to be learned from the Book of Revelation it's important to remember that some of the content has happened, some of it is happening, and some have yet to happen. At any rate, it's a great treatise on the ongoing struggle between good and evil.

Several times over the years in teaching situations I've opened the sessions up for questions and discussions about anything in the Bible they'd like to talk about. Without fail the questions almost immediately go to the Book of Revelation. And, in those few times that I did that, I almost as quickly wished I hadn't opened it up at all! I say that because there are so many questions that I can't answer. In fact, the book brings up many questions that nobody can accurately answer due to the structure, scope, broad diversity and the ongoing prophetic nature of the book.

Eschatology, the study of "end times," is especially interesting to most people because they want to know how this whole thing is going to end up. There are hundreds of differing and conflicting opinions of just how that's going to happen. And the truth of it is that no one knows quite for sure about all of it except Jesus and the Father. Many people hold an obsession about end times and often get in the ditch thinking about nothing else but that. That's a huge problem if you ask me. When I tell people that I'm not obsessed with the end times, they have a problem with that. They ask, "Where's your urgency?" To which my answer always is, "My urgency is preaching, teaching and imparting the kingdom of

God to anyone and everyone the Lord puts in my path today. That's my urgency!" Since no one knows the day or the hour of Jesus's return, I refuse to stand around and argue with someone about when that's going to happen! I will also say, unequivocally, that the people I see that are obsessed with the end times are NOT changing the world!

So, when you're reading and studying the Book of Revelation let the Spirit guide you and speak to you. Use some common sense and don't get in the ditch where the end times are concerned.

THE GREAT PARADOXES
OF THE BIBLE

"I have found the paradox, that if I love until it hurts, then there is no hurt, but only more love."

— Mother Teresa

A paradox is a seemingly absurd or self-contradictory statement or proposition that when investigated or explained may prove to be well founded or true.

The New Testament is laced with, what I call, kingdom logic. Kingdom logic very often differs vastly from human logic. There are laws, or rules, of the kingdom of God that defy our own logic, and in many cases, defy even common sense. No matter how absurd they may sound these spiritual (kingdom) laws, when adhered to, never fail to bring life and to prove their content to be valid. They are eternal in nature. It's only when we begin to get a handle on understanding the kingdom of God that these rules of the kingdom begin to make sense. Jesus often spoke very profound truths by using a paradox. The most comprehensive work to date on the paradoxes in the Bible was penned by Henry Clay Trumbull who died in 1903. His book, *Practical Paradoxes, Or, Truth in Contradictions*, is an exposé on the many truths in the Bible that appear to be, at least on the surface, very contradictory to how the human mind thinks and reasons. For instance, according to these kingdom laws, giving is getting; scattering is gaining; holding is losing; having nothing is possessing all things; dying is living. He who is weak is strong; he who loses his life will find it. And, there are many more paradoxes throughout the Bible that not only test the boundaries of conventional thinking but which find their fullness of truth and meaning, only, in renewed kingdom thinking, reasoning and logic.

The Pharisees in Jesus's day displayed a perfect case in point. Jesus said, "He who is greatest among you will be your servant." Because they rejected Jesus, they weren't able to understand the things He said to them. He further declared, "Father, You have hidden these things from the wise and prudent and revealed them to babes." So, clearly, one needn't be an academic genius to understand the paradoxes that Jesus taught.

As you read your Bible, notice the things Jesus says that seem to defy logic. Embrace those paradoxes, put them to the test by faith, and you'll be amazed at how the Lord responds to your action.

ENGAGE:

Look up the following verses and identify the paradox present there.

- Luke 6:38

- 2 Corinthians 12:10

- John 12:25

- James 2:5

SYMBOLS, TYPES, AND SHADOWS

"God wants to speak into areas of your life you have never even considered. He wants to give you words and wisdom you didn't think were possible. He desires to do exceedingly more than you can hope or expect."

—Margaret Feinberg

The Bible is a truly magnificent Book, to say the least. It is, after all, God's Word. And, while much of it can be interpreted, and understood from, a strictly literal standpoint it's also important to understand that it's laced and accented with all kinds of imagery as to further display its mysterious nature. An ongoing understanding of Biblical imagery is essential to any serious Bible student in that there are literally hundreds of symbols and types that have significant meanings. It's almost like going on an adventurous treasure hunt when you begin to get a glimpse of these things.

Time and space prohibit me from going into great detail in talking about symbols, types, and shadows as there are so many but I'll start by saying that you already know a few of those important Biblical symbols. For instance, from the beginning of the Book, a lamb is symbolic of Jesus; a dove is symbolic of the Holy Spirit, a serpent is symbolic of Satan, and the list goes on and on. There are literally hundreds (maybe more) of these in Scripture. When you begin to look closer at the symbols and types and start to notice them, it will give you much greater insight and clarity into what you're reading.

God has ingeniously woven this imagery throughout Scripture to help us further understand His will and His way. Some of the different symbols and images include such things as people, nations, sounds, colors, animals, fruit, vegetables, rocks, smoke, creatures, snakes, places, numbers and many many more. I have only listed these to spark your curiosity. I encourage you to pursue a knowledge of the symbols, types, and shadows. You'll be glad you did!

These two literary works below are some that I have found to be especially helpful to me. They're both user friendly. I highly recommend them as you pursue an understanding of Biblical symbols, types, shadows, and imagery.

- *Interpreting the Symbols and Types*, Kevin Conner
- *Dictionary of Biblical Imagery*, Leland Ryken

FIRST THE NATURAL,
THEN THE SPIRITUAL

However, the spiritual is not first, but the natural, and afterward the spiritual. The first man was of the earth, made of dust; the second Man is the Lord from heaven.

1 Cor 15:46-48

In Paul's letter to the Corinthians, he disclosed a key to Biblical interpretation and study. Many things that we encounter in the Old Testament under the Old Covenant only find their fulfillment when we begin to see them from a spiritual standpoint. Many things are "typified" in the Old that find their true meaning in the New Covenant. For instance, the incredible Red Sea crossing by the displaced Israelites is a type and shadow of water baptism. The Israelites were leaving Egypt, which means "bondage." They went through the waters and up on the other side to a new life. Can you see the picture of baptism here? There is the principle; first the natural, then the spiritual.

Another example and there are hundreds, is that under the Old Covenant sacrifices were to be brought to the altar to honor the Lord. Those sacrifices varied according to the commandments of the Lord for that particular covenant. The sacrifices might be sheep, goats, or cattle. They might even be crops, fruit, and vegetables. But under the New Covenant, our sacrifices are spiritual, rather than natural sacrifices. In Romans 12, Paul encourages the believers there to offer their …

… bodies as a living sacrifice, holy, acceptable to God, which is your reasonable service.

Another great example of this is found in Hebrews 13:15-16:

Therefore by Him let us continually offer the sacrifice of praise to God, that is, the fruit of our lips, giving thanks to His name.

Abraham had an amazing encounter with God. God told him to, "get out of your country, from your family and from your father's house." The Bible records that Abraham did just that. "He went out not

135

knowing where he was going." If you think about it, we're to do the same thing, only from a spiritual standpoint! We must come out from under those things that have defined us (hometown, family, generational way of thinking), and go out by faith following the Lord! First the natural, then the spiritual!

Probably the most vivid picture of this principle is the story of the sacrificial lamb during the Jewish Passover feast. Obviously, this points to Jesus. Every Jewish family was to take a lamb that was without spot or blemish, (Jesus = Sinless), slay the lamb and apply the blood of the lamb on the sides and upper part of the door. When the angel of death came through during the night and saw the blood, those households were spared from the death of their firstborn sons. It's a beautiful picture of this principle, first the natural, then the spiritual. Jesus was "THE" sacrificial lamb, and His blood cleanses us from all unrighteousness!

You will begin to see these examples all over your Bible. If you're like me, it makes the entire Bible reading experience more enjoyable. The Bible is a marvelous literary work, and there are principles and mysteries just waiting to be found throughout the whole Book!

HIDDEN TRUTH

"I thank you, Father, Lord of heaven and earth, that you have hidden these things from the wise and prudent and revealed them to babes."

— Jesus

The Bible is full of Truth. Even a casual reading of a chapter, passage or verse can reveal amazing insight to some of the many questions life brings. But, I have noticed over the years that there is also an incredible amount of profound truth found just under the surface of that casual reading. There are things you don't immediately see, but once you begin to inspect more closely, the Word can come alive in even greater ways. In that respect, "yes," there are things that are hidden.

It brings up a valid question, "Does God "hide" His Truth from us?". That's a very good question. I think to adequately answer that question we must attempt to look at it from His standpoint. If He actually does want us to know the Truth it doesn't make much sense, at least from a Father's standpoint, that He would hide it from us. I mean, why would He do that?!

One of the most rewarding things in mine and Julie's life right now is the joy we get from our grandchildren. We have nine (soon to be 10!) of the best-lookin', smartest, unique (I could go on and on, but you get the point! LOL) little kids you've ever seen. They're all within close proximity to us which we consider a huge blessing. So, it's often that we're all together. I will admit it can get pretty wild and hectic at times but, again, that's one of the things we love most about it.

On Easter, we'll gather our entire bunch. There's usually about twenty of us, often including a few extras. We'll have a big feast of some kind for lunch and then as soon as lunch is over we'll hide the Easter eggs. Some of our grandkids have outgrown that part of the festivities, and help us adults hide the eggs, but several are still small enough to really enjoy it. Take the youngest two for example; Knox and Timber are just past two years old, and nothing thrills them more on this particular holiday than finding an Easter egg. They love it. We could easily hide the eggs in places the little ones would never find them. But where's the fun in that?! The fun part for us is to see them find the eggs! I can almost see the delight and excitement in their little faces now.

If you're wondering what this little story has to do with what we're talking about, here it is. When we hide those eggs we're not hiding them "FROM" the little ones, we're hiding the eggs "FOR" them! Get it?! We want them to find the eggs!

For there is nothing hidden which will not be revealed, nor has anything been kept secret but that it should come to light. If anyone has ears to hear, let him hear.

Mark 4:22-23

With this thought in mind, along with the above verse, one can only surmise that those things that are "hidden" are, only hidden, that we might discover them!

Call to me and I will answer you, and will tell you great and hidden things that you have no known.

Jeremiah 33:3

There are so many things hidden just under the surface of what you see written in the Bible. You should go looking! And, when you're thinking about hidden truth remember, the Father doesn't hide that Truth from you, He hides it for you!!

SECTION 6

CONTEXT—IT'S EVERYTHING!

The vigor of our spiritual life will be in exact proportion to the place held by the Bible in our life and thoughts."

—George Muller

When I was only a year or two along in my new walk with the Lord, I was invited to go to San Antonio, Texas to a week-long event called The Keys of Knowledge Seminar. The seminar consisted of 8-9 hour days in learning methods and principles of studying the Bible. It was the equivalent of an entire college semester of training. It was intense and full of extremely helpful principles in studying the Bible. The Seminar was taught by a brilliant Bible teacher by the name of Kevin Conner, an Australian, who taught us many valuable things in that short time, things that have proven to be incredibly vital for me as a Bible teacher.

One of those very important Bible study principles was the Contextual Principle. We were taught the utter importance of context. What is the context? Who are the particular scriptures or verses directed to? What were the cultural conditions and ramifications during that time? After that portion of the seminar, two things emerged out of all the information we received on the subject of context:

1) Work to understand what the context is!

2) Do Not take Scripture or verse out of context to make your point!

It's stated in other places in this book, but it bears repeating. You can make the Bible say anything you want it to say, but that is not our goal as students of the Word! If we're to handle the Word of God wisely, if we're to "rightly divide the word of Truth," if we're to preach and teach the "whole counsel of God," if we're to be guardians of, and trusted purveyors, of the Truth we must keep His Word in context!

WHAT ARE YOU TRYING TO MAKE THE BIBLE SAY?

"The truth is, it doesn't matter what a verse means to me, to you, or to anyone else. All that matters is what the verse means!"
—John F. MacArthur Jr

One of the classic mistakes much of the Christian community makes is to try to make the Bible say what they want it to say. I see and hear this happening far too often. This is a no-no of epic proportions. It's actually possible to take Scripture out of context and make the Bible say just about anything you want it to say. But, that's not at all what our goal is as we read the Bible. Our goal is to draw the pure, unadulterated truth from the Word in its original meaning so we will ultimately have a clear and accurate view of what's been written.

Someone made the observation in a joking manner that the problem with this kind of errant method, in taking Scripture and verses out of context, could lead to nonsense such as this:

"Judas went out from the temple and hanged himself" (Mt 27:5);

"And, Jesus said, "Go, and do likewise" (Luke 10:37).

That's an extreme example, but when you take Scripture out of context that's what could happen! And, while I'm joking, the example does make a profound point as it relates to what I'm saying.

We must approach our Bible reading and study with a clean heart, pure motives with absolutely no agenda to prove our point or to validate our little pet doctrines. We must allow the Word to speak to our hearts in that clean, pure, unadulterated Truth that it's purposed for. Jesus has promised that the Holy Spirit will lead us into all Truth. For that to happen, we must stop trying to make the Bible say what we want it to say!

EVERYTHING IS WRITTEN FOR US, BUT NOT EVERYTHING IS WRITTEN TO US

"When you read a verse in the Bible ask yourself, "What does this verse mean?" Then ask: "What does it mean for me?" When that is answered ask yourself again: "Is that all it means?" And do not leave it until you are quite sure that is all it means for the present."

—R.A. Torrey

One of the classic mistakes that most Bible readers make is to make everything they read personal to them. It's important to realize that while everything that's written is there for your benefit, everything is not written, specifically, "to" you.

There was a guy that went to our church for a few months. He was beginning to connect, loved the family and loved the message of the house. Nothing he didn't like. But, all of a sudden he disappeared. I happened onto him a month later and told him we'd been missing him. He said, "I love it there but one Sunday you had a woman come up and pray over the offering, and the Bible says that women should keep silent in the church. What you're doing is not Biblical. So, I'm not coming back." It's a classic misunderstanding of what the Word actually says. In that particular context, in Corinth, the women were causing a problem in the corporate gathering. Every time the church came together, they were speaking out of turn and causing a disturbance. When Paul said that he was speaking directly to that particular, local, problem, he was not saying that women should not have an important place in the church. Much to the contrary! When you look at the entire New Testament, you see that women had a very important place in the plan of God. For instance, Priscilla obviously had an apostolic anointing. Phoebe was a deaconess. And there are many others who played a significant role in the advancement of the kingdom of God in the early church. It should be expected in these days as well. For women to be disqualified in being an important and functional part of the church today is a gross misinterpretation of what the Word is saying. It is sad that many groups have interpreted this as how it should be today. As a result of this kind of faulty interpretation and thinking the church has been limited in the blessing of anointed women ministering and making a difference in the daily affairs of the church.

There are dozens of legitimate examples, but one that stands clear is Paul's letters to Timothy. In the two short, but extremely important, letters to young Timothy Paul gives some practical and profound instructions to his son in the faith. Those letters can give anyone some very sound advice in living the Christian life. We can, and should, take Paul's words and apply them to our own lives. But, it's clear. The letters are not to us; they are to Timothy! We should glean from the rich wisdom that's contained in the letters but not enforce them as "law," or legalism, on ourselves or the ones we might be ministering to.

The Bible is full of incredible insight, practical wisdom and help for just about anything you can think of but it's important to remember that while everything is "for" us, not everything is "to" us!

When you read your Bible ask the Lord what He wants you to learn from it. He will be quick to show you. He won't leave you in suspense. He won't leave you hanging!

ALL YOUR ANSWERS ARE
NOT IN THE BIBLE!

"Everything in the Bible is true, but all that is true is not in the Bible."

—Jack Taylor

As you certainly know by now, the Bible is full of incredible stories, facts, principles, and information. Information that, without a doubt, is relevant for virtually every imaginable area of our lives. And, while the Bible is complete in its scope, there are things in life that you just can't find answers for in the Bible. Even as I write this I sense that there will be several, maybe more, that will reject this chapter altogether because of what I just said; some might even reject the whole book, for that matter. Don't do that! Read on with an open mind, and heart, then decide for yourself after you read this important chapter!

To start with I want to say that God, absolutely, does speak through the Bible. That's a no-brainer! I would never, ever deny that! He does that, and I'm constantly "hearing" Him about things that pertain to me and the things I am concerned with. Many times He will speak specifically through the Word things that are very personal to you and your situations. But not always.

The Father has a myriad of ways in which He speaks to us in addition to His written Word. It's futile to try and list all those ways but here are a few to consider. He speaks to us through dreams and visions; through words of knowledge and words of wisdom; through the elements and nature; through other people; through personal prophecy; and my personal favorite, that "still small voice."

I often tell people, "The Bible gives us many of the generalities of life, but He has saved many of the specifics so He can tell them to you personally!" Let me give you a simple example; Let's say that you are dating a person and as is normal, you begin to wonder if this is "The" person you're supposed to marry. You may look from Genesis to Revelation and not find that answer. (Disclaimer: But make no mistake, God can give you Scriptural confirmation about this kind of thing, He just doesn't always do it that way) So, in this particular situation, what do you do? My advice is that you take it to the Lord. Begin to pray that God will speak to you in some way so you'll know exactly what to do.

When you stop and think, it begins to make perfect sense. It's just like the Father to "seal up" some of the specific details of our life so that the only way we can find them out is to go to Him! I sincerely believe it's His design. He wants to interact with you. He wants to reveal Himself to you. He wants to show you how much He loves you. And, yes, He will answer your prayers, but the real payoff is that you'll experience His presence and His love, firsthand! That, my friend, is life altering! It's one of the things you're going to love about Him the most!

Incidentally, you can trust in the reality that if God speaks something to your Spirit, it will never contradict what is written in His Word, and it will always be consistent with the nature of the Father.

As you read your Bible, you're going to find answer after answer to many of the questions you encounter in life. But, don't forget that the Father wants to be even more intimate with you as He speaks mysteries and secrets about you and for you that can't be found anywhere else.

RIGHTLY DIVIDING THE WORD OF TRUTH

"The mediocre teacher tells. The good teacher explains. The superior teacher demonstrates. The great teacher inspires."

—William A. Ward

In Paul's second letter to young Timothy he encouraged him, "Be diligent to present yourself approved to God, a worker who does not need to be ashamed, rightly dividing the word of truth." 2 Tim 2:15-16 What does it mean to "rightly divide the word of truth?"

Paul took great care to teach and impart to Timothy the unmistakable, dire importance of teaching the Word in a serious and mature manner. That would include not to err, or turn away from the Truth, as well as accurately and responsibly handling the Word in a straightforward and uncompromising way.

In another place, Paul, writing to the elders in Ephesus says, "For I did not shrink from declaring to you the whole counsel of God." Plagued with challenges of every kind including being ridiculed, beaten and left for dead, snakebitten, and shipwrecked, Paul still managed to "run the race" and "fight the good fight!" By declaring the whole counsel of God Paul managed to convey and communicate the whole of God's revelation, leaving nothing of importance out. This would include subjects such as equipping them for the work of the ministry, helping them to understand the written Word, God's purpose for their own redemption as well as His plan for the redemption of all mankind. He must have surely convinced them of the futility of a world, or of a life without Jesus and that salvation was easy to attain for them all. He must have told them of the transforming power of the Holy Spirit using his own life as an example. He must have imparted to them a sense of destiny and that the Father had a unique plan for each of them. Paul never balked in teaching them about Jesus and the resurrection. To sum it all up, Paul told them everything that the Lord had entrusted to him. He taught them the "whole counsel of God!"

"ITCHING EARS"

"We are more likely to catch glimpses of truth when we allow what we think and believe to be tested."

—Choan-Seng Song

The time will come when they will not endure sound doctrine, but according to their own desires, because they have itching ears, they will heap up for themselves teachers; and they will turn their ears away from the truth, and be turned aside to fables.

2 Tim 4:3-5

In Paul's second letter to Timothy, he warned him that there was a time coming when the people would "not endure sound doctrine." Earlier in that same letter, he encouraged him to "rightly divide" the word of truth. Paul took great care to impart to Timothy the dire necessity of respecting the integrity of the Word of God. He called it the "pillar and ground of the truth."

People with itching ears pick out parts of the Word and build their entire doctrinal stance around that. That's a serious mistake! Any time you make "anything," everything you're in danger of being in error in your understanding of the Word! We should teach, and be open to, the "whole counsel of God!"

I have found that even today there are those who want, only, their version of the truth preached. They have arrived at certain conclusions and have decided that's the way it is, and they're intolerant to anyone teaching anything to the contrary. In that way, they fall into the category of having "itching ears." They want to heap up for themselves teachers who will tickle their ears, those that will solidify their stance, and prop up their little "pet" doctrines—teachers that only teach the way they believe.

I've found in listening to other teachers that I don't always agree 100%. There are even times that I don't agree with much at all but rather than reject everything that the teacher is saying I have learned to listen and allow the Holy Spirit to teach me. I have learned to allow the teaching gift of another to sharpen me even if I find myself in disagreement on certain issues.

The truth is you can arrive at any number of Biblical conclusions, and without trying too hard, you can find another verse that seems to challenge the authenticity of it. I think the Lord likes that. I think He likes us to be challenged and to have to think our way around what the discrepancy between the two verses might be. It's as if there's always a little "friction" around many of the truths we find in the Bible. Again, I think the Lord likes this. It's a way to keep us growing and to keep us from getting static, stale and rigid in our growth. And, it keeps us from "setting up camp" around any one particular doctrine.

Do you have "itching ears?" If you refuse to listen to anyone else's opinion or perspective on a subject, if you are prone to completely turn off another teacher who's teaching something that challenges your position, or if you only want to sit under teachers that are only teaching "your version" of the truth; you just might have! It's definitely something to be cautious of.

ARGUING SCRIPTURE

"Let go of your attachment to being right, and suddenly your mind is more open. You're able to benefit from the unique viewpoints of others, without being crippled by your own judgment."
—Ralph Marston

I get opportunities to do it all the time. I never take the bait. There's not much I enjoy more than a good discussion on the Word. We have some incredible talks around my office, most of them unplanned, that cause me to think. I have a great group of friends, and we all enjoy challenging one another about certain Scriptural topics. It's rare that we all agree a hundred percent on any single topic. We all have an opinion and to be completely honest everyone has a valid point. It's very healthy. We can get pretty brisk in our discussions at times, but it's never from a domineering, manipulative or harsh argumentative, standpoint. We all come away with a much better perspective than we started with. And we all remain close friends. But, the thing that's common among us is that not a single one of us think we have all the truth. In fact, our bunch is a great example of what I've encouraged you to be, we're learners!

As much as I love those discussions, I don't feel the need to argue Scripture to try to prove my point with anyone, and as I said earlier, the opportunity is often present for me to do that. Many self-professed Bible scholars cross a line where they think they know it all concerning certain topics and they seem to be on a mission to persuade everyone else to move on over to their position. They're quick to judge you to be wrong if your stance is different than theirs, which mine nearly always is. More often than not it's a pride thing. They want to impress everyone with what they think they know. The Bible gives a clear disclaimer about knowledge; it puffs up! Nothing at all wrong with knowledge, as long as you know the dangers.

I'm very serious about the Word. I want to be correct in my understanding of it, and I want to be correct in the way that I communicate it to everyone else. That's very important to me. I approach my responsibility as a teacher of the Word with the greatest amount of seriousness. I do have strong opinions and convictions about Scriptural topics. My opinions are a result of thirty-five years of studying the Bible and sitting under great teachers of the Bible and asking a lot of good questions. But, I have found that over the years I can be at peace with where someone is on a Scriptural topic, even when it differs from mine. I may not be at peace with being there myself, but that's OK. The key for all of us is whether or not we can change in our positions. I can, but some people cannot. So, I don't at all feel the need to pressure them to come over to my way of thinking.

Someone said it this way, "Discussion is an exchange of knowledge; argument is an exchange of ignorance." You're going to get the opportunity often to argue the Scripture. My advice is, "Don't!"

SECTION 7

READ THROUGH THE BIBLE IN A YEAR?

"It is not the quantity that is read, but the manner of reading, that yields us profit"

—Jean Guyon and Francois Fenelon (17th Century)

I may go a little off the map for some of you here, but I think it's important to address the subject from a little different perspective than you might normally expect.

Lots of people have done it. There are plans on just about every Christian and church website you encounter on how to read through the Bible in a year. I have a friend who lives an hour away who's read through the Bible every year, now, for over 40 years straight! That's commendable; I wouldn't argue that point at all. I could only guess that it would deepen your understanding as well as your respect for the Book. I say, I could only guess the ways you might benefit, because I've never done it even one time. And, it's not found anywhere on my bucket list of things to do. I guess that could change, and I'm open to the Lord if He were to direct me that way. But, at the moment, "I ain't feelin' it!" I'm sure some of my readers will have a difficult time digesting that, but it's true.

The question would immediately arise as to why I would take such a position, seeing that thousands of others have committed to it, followed through and say they are blessed because of it. Again, I wouldn't argue that point. But, for me the answer is simple. Quantity of Bible reading doesn't always equate to "quality" reading.

It's not fair to say "all," but it seems to me that a lot of people I've encountered like to tell you about their feat of reading through Bible in a year kind of like they've earned some sort of spiritual merit badge. That's OK with me, and I don't want to hurt any body's feelings, but it always leaves me wondering how much has really been accomplished. I'd rather see someone spend a year in Luke 15, for instance, than to see them try to tackle the "whole enchilada." The Holy Spirit is good enough at what He does to help each of those readers get some profound wisdom from their time in the Word. And, there's no doubt about it, the Father will take any opportunity He gets to establish, confirm and solidify His Word in our lives.

If spiritual growth is important to you, I would encourage you to slow down, get a grasp on the context, paying special attention to every word, and giving those words a chance to land and settle in your spirit while at the same time being sensitive to the Holy Spirit as He quickens (brings alive) those words in your heart. I believe you'll be glad you did!

THE BIBLE ON CD DILEMMA

And because you are sons, God has sent forth the Spirit of His Son into your hearts, crying out, 'Abba, Father!' Therefore you are no longer a slave but a son, and if a son, then an heir of God through Christ.

—Gal 4:6-7

A close friend of mine gave a mutual friend, who was not a churchgoer, a set of Bible CDs. After a couple of weeks, our friend came by my house and brought the CDs back. I could tell he wasn't at peace, so I questioned him about it. "Did you not like them?" I'll never forget his answer. "No," I didn't like them." I couldn't figure out where he was coming from. I asked him, "Why?" He said, "Obviously, you can do this stuff but I can't!" When I listen to them, they just remind me how bad I am. They remind me that I'm not good enough. So, No, I don't want them. They're discouraging to me. I don't want to listen to them anymore."

That started me thinking. Why would he respond to the Word like that? At the beginning, I couldn't understand it. Here's what I learned. When we read, or in our friend's case "hear," the Bible without the understanding that God is our Father we can easily take the words of scripture as criticism or condemnation. When that's the case, it's easy to perceive that God is pointing out all the things that are wrong with us; all the things that keep us from being a good person. But, that's not something that a good Father would do. In fact, it's far from it!

One of my favorite authors, E. Stanley Jones, stated it this way. "There are many things we read in the Bible that we receive as commandments when, in all actuality, they are simply, invitations." For instance, when the Word encourages us to "be holy like He is holy" if we interpret that as a commandment it would seem fairly obvious that all of us would fall monumentally short of fulfilling that in our daily lives. But, on the other hand, if we would just accept that as an invitation, then it would give us something to live up to; something to shoot for, something to live toward rather than receiving it as something that we cannot do or something that we have consistently failed in. I think a right perception of this could be quite revolutionary in our journey of being conformed into His image. The Bible says that we have been "born again of "incorruptible" seed." The seed of perfection has been germinated in us! One of the great teachers of our generation, Bob Mumford, says it this way: "All the

DNA of the oak tree is contained in the little acorn." It's the same for you and me.

It's important to realize that the Bible doesn't instruct us to do anything that's not doable. In fact, everything is do-able, but more often than not we will need the help of the Holy Spirit to help us flesh it out.

So, be careful when you read your Bible that you don't take what's meant to be an encouragement and turn it into condemnation.

A WORKING KNOWLEDGE
OF THE BIBLE

"You gotta get in the Word, 'til the Word gets in you."

—Andy Taylor

When my life made a dramatic turn in 1984, my wife, Julie had just recently bought *The New King James Version*. I basically took the Bible from her! I'm not sure she even gave me permission to take it, but I guess she thought that maybe I'd actually read it, and that would be a good thing! And, read it I did! When I got into that *NKJV Bible*, I couldn't quit. It was easier to understand than the *King James Version* for me. And, as I found out later, it remains very close to the *KJV* without the cumbersome language of the 1600s. At any rate, it was the version of the Bible I first became acquainted with, and I've stuck with it for 35 years now.

I was raised on an extremely remote ranch in the Texas Panhandle. We were 35 miles from a town of any size. (Canadian, Texas, Pop. 3000). And, as the old adage goes, "where we lived wasn't on the way to anywhere!" But after I began my walk with the Lord, a strange phenomenon began to take place. Many of my friends from my "old life", beer drinkers, partiers, etc., started showing up at my house, out there in the middle of nowhere. It was really amazing how often it happened. These guys were opening up about their lives and their problems asking me what they should do. Even though I had been immersed in the Bible, I had hardly any answers for them. I just knew that if God could fix my life, He could surely fix theirs! Their extremely diverse, and broad range of problems and questions caused me to dig in the Word for answers. I'd go home at night and dig, and dig, and dig to find the answers. And, now after 35 years, I don't think I've ever heard the same question twice. I can see clearly now that it was the Lord's way of helping me find my way around the Word.

I had to put that old Bible aside for a new one several years back. Its pages are worn and torn. They're marked with half a dozen different colors of pens, pencils, and highlighters. The cover is faded and coming apart. Mark 1 & 2 are completely missing. Cole, my third son, at about age two had ripped them out, wadded them up in a little ball and was about to put them into his mouth when I discovered them.

I learned my way around the Bible by looking for answers for my friends. Through all that I developed, what I call, a "working knowledge" of the Bible. I had no idea in those days that the Lord would use me in any ministry capacity at all. Never dreamed of it! But He knew! And, how He trained me in the Book has been invaluable to me in being a leader, counselor, and teacher of the Word.

You can do the same. Whenever your friends or family have a serious life event, grab your Bible and start looking. Keep looking until you find an answer or a verse that would encourage them. Just do that! Keep doing it, and you'll develop a working knowledge of the Bible, yourself!

PRAY THE WORD, DECLARE THE WORD, MINISTER THE WORD, CELEBRATE THE WORD

"Prayer is beyond any question the highest activity of the human soul. Man is at his greatest and highest when upon his knees he comes face to face with God."

—Martyn Lloyd-Jones

Pray the Word

One thing you'll want to consider as you grow in the Word is to incorporate the words in the Bible into your regular prayer routine. Praying the Word can add a powerful dimension to your prayers. When I'm praying, I might say, "Lord, your Word says that I can do all things through Christ." He knows what the Word says, so you're not reminding Him of it. He doesn't need to be reminded! (LOL)But, more importantly, you're praying by faith what He has recorded in His Word. You're coming into agreement with what is written! His Word, mixed with your faith as you pray, brings a much more powerful component to your prayer life. Start now to incorporate the Word of God in your prayer time!

Pray the Word!

Declare the Word

There is a great degree of power available when you declare the Word of God in any given situation. To declare is to just speak the Word out loud. This is beneficial at any time but particularly helpful and powerful during those times you might be discouraged or in a spiritual battle. The Lord "inhabits" the praises (declarations) of His people. It has been my experience in those times I am discouraged or having a bad day that when I declare the Word my mood and demeanor changes, and it doesn't take long! Sometimes it's instantaneous! Very often when I get up in the morning, I'll declare, "This is the day that the Lord has made; I will rejoice and be glad in it!" Carpe diem! That's how you seize the day, friend before the day seizes you!

Declare the Word!

Minister the Word

For those, and I encourage everyone to, who intend on following the Lord to another level in personal ministry it's a wise thing to minister the Word. If we only give people our advice, in the final analysis, we'll only be secular counselors. Our counsel, as good as it might be, can only go so far. But ministering the Word of God actually has the life-giving, miracle-working power of God on it! When you are ministering to someone, speak out the Word for that specific situation. You'll find that the Holy Spirit will show up and give life to the Word you're voicing. It makes sense as you're learning about the Bible to memorize some of those verses that have had an impact on you. When you're ministering to others, you'll discover that those things will start to come up in your mind. Also, when you minister the Word to someone else, they will hear the words you speak over them and more often than not they'll remember what you said. Remember, the Word of God is quick (alive), and powerful! It's one of the great weapons of warfare we've been given. The Bible calls the Word of God the "sword" of the Spirit. When we wield that sword, the enemy cowers under the power of God. You're destined to be victorious in all the affairs of this life! The Bible says, "You are more than a conqueror through Christ Jesus"!

It is interesting to note that when Jesus was tempted by the devil in the wilderness that, three times, He declared, "It is written!" There's a "key" for you! The Word of God is a powerful weapon anytime you find yourself under attack. And, you can do the same when you are ministering the Word over someone else. Your enemy, the devil, knows the Word and he has no recourse but to retreat at your declaration!

Minister the Word!

Celebrate the Word

By now, you've been given, in utterly simple fashion, principles which can and will guide you along as you become a serious student of the Word of God. As you continue to apply these simple principles to your Bible reading, your comprehension and understanding will grow exponentially. The Bible declares that the "seed" is the Word of God. As you allow the seeds of the Word to take root in your mind, will, and emotions, you'll not only be established in His Word, you'll also find yourself being established in the faith! What's more, you'll find your true identity as a chosen son or daughter of the Most High God! Your life will never be the same!

Celebrate the Word!

"LET NOT MANY OF YOU BE TEACHERS"

"Avowed atheists are not a tenth as dangerous as those preachers who scatter doubt and stab at faith."

—C.H. Spurgeon

In James's short, but power-packed letter he issued a strict admonition to the readers. He said, "Let not many of you become teachers, knowing that we shall receive a stricter judgment." What could he be referring to? Is he telling us not to be teachers of the Word? Probably not. In fact, I don't think he is saying that at all. What I do believe he wants to do is emphasize the seriousness of being a teacher of the Bible. Today, as in the first century, there are many false teachers roaming around. It's a serious infraction, to say the least. The world is in need of those who have an extreme respect and reverence of the Word and a deep conviction to be true Bible interpreters; those who are determined to mine the Truth and convey it as it was originally intended.

It's not rare to happen onto those who have learned a few Bible principles, think they know it all and have decided to start teaching others. It seems harmless at face value. I've observed some of these people over the years and how they seek to impress new converts or those who know little to no Scripture at all. If you've seen a picture or video of baby birds waiting with their little mouths open ready to devour whatever the momma bird brings them then you can get a picture of how a new convert who's hungry for the Word might be. The last thing that needs to happen is for some immature, self-professing, egotistical Bible teacher to start stuffing trash down them. This is an offense of the highest order if you ask me. It appears that it was equally important to Jesus; He told the Pharisees in Matt 18:6 "Whoever causes one of these little ones who believe in Me to sin, it would be better for him if a millstone were hung around his neck, and he were drowned in the depth of the sea." It can take a lifetime to deprogram someone from faulty, incorrect teaching! Deciding to be a Bible teacher without being mature is like the guy that took one karate lesson and then decided to put it to use; he quickly found out that he learned just enough to get his rear kicked!

One of the first and foremost ingredients in becoming a trusted Bible teacher is to sit under great teachers. I've had the blessing and good fortune to have been able to do that in my life. Some of those who have impacted me the most are mentioned in the front of this book. But, it's important to note that I made it a priority to seek out those who were solid, seasoned, respected and consistent in their teaching. I credit many of these people in helping me to become a respected teacher as well.

I sincerely believe if James could speak to you today he would definitely stick to the tenets of his original letter. But, I also think he'd encourage you to move forward, to dig in, to mature, to be seasoned and apply yourself to become an incredible teacher of the Word. The world is deeply in need of those who'll do that.

It is a serious thing to become a teacher of the Bible. It should be approached with the greatest degree of seriousness and integrity. The simple, practical principles you find in this book will help you not only, understand the Bible better but become someone that can be trusted to teach others also.

OH, BY THE WAY—A WORD TO LEADERS

In working with Pastors and training church leaders for over 30 years, I'm often amazed and somewhat surprised to find that many of them don't have good, solid methods and principles for studying the Bible. I think you'll agree that's an unhealthy scenario. And, it happens more often than you might think. As leaders, we should work to be skilled in 'mining' the Truth from the Word. Solid, proven methods and principles diligently exercised, along with the Holy Spirit's help, is a guarantee that what we're teaching will be accurate and powerful with the potential to change individual lives as well as entire nations.

In the process of writing this book, I've talked to several pastors and ministry leaders. It's consistent, and we all agree that most of the people sitting in our services on any given Sunday don't know how to read their Bible. In fact, that's how this book came to be in the first place. We agree that up to 80%-90% of the rank and file of church attendees don't have a clue where to start or how to study their Bible systematically. Think of how beneficial it would be for every person under your leadership to be able to glean more from their Bible reading. The results and momentum it might bring for you could very well be revolutionary!

If training our people in the skills needed to be proficient in Bible reading and application is important to you, this little, easy to understand, book might be just what you need to spark the fire. I have intentionally made the chapters short, easy to understand but full of concentrated truth.

I'm suggesting we start a revolution! A revolution that would enable and equip every single person in the Body of Christ to read and study their Bible with confidence and consistency. Here are a few ways you can help to ignite that revolution:

- Teach the principles from the pulpit—The whole "family" gets it at once
- Start a class—Because of the simplicity of this book virtually anyone could lead a class
- Start small groups—Help your people learn the Bible and foster the family element at the same time
- Donate the books to jails, prisons, or drug/alcohol rehab centers

You never know what just one person might do who begins to understand their Bible clearly. Whatever method you choose to proceed you can be confident in knowing that you are changing the world for the better!

SECTION 8

A CONTEMPLATIVE LIFE

"Give every truth time to send down deep roots into the heart."
—Francois Fenelon & Jean Guyon

There have been a few down through the generations who have opted out of the normal Christian life for, what I call, a contemplative life. Those who live the contemplative life are devoted primarily to prayer, worship, study, and meditation of the Word of God—sometimes, even in a monastery or convent living with others who are like-minded. While prayer is an essential component for all believers, these contemplatives feel called to make their entire lives about prayer in solitude, silence, and community.

One of my favorite authors, Henri J.M. Nouwen, often refers to the Desert Fathers. The Desert Fathers were early Christian hermits and monks who lived mainly in the desert of Egypt around the third century. The most well-known was Anthony the Great. By the time of his death in 356 AD, thousands of monks and nuns had been drawn to living in the desert following his example. The Desert Fathers had a major influence on the development of early Christianity.

Realistically speaking, probably no one reading this book will choose a separated life like those of the Desert Fathers and others like them, but there is much to be learned from those that did! Here are some books that have been a blessing to me. I highly recommend these authors and books as they will give you a glimpse into the contemplative world. They're short, easy to read, full of experiential wisdom and will help you develop some of the meditation and reflection habits of the contemplatives as you learn to let the Word "marinate" in your spirit.

- *Experiencing the Depths of Jesus Christ*, Jean Guyon
- *The Seeking Heart*, Francois Fenelon
- *Practicing His Presence*, Brother Lawrence

LECTIO DIVINA

"If meditation is to be fruitful, it must be followed by devoted prayer, and the sweetness of contemplation may be called the effect of prayer."

—Guigo II, the Carthusian

If you're like I was that term means absolutely nothing to you. In reading a book recently by an author who over the last few years has become one of my very favorites, Dallas Willard (I highly suggest you check out any of his books!), I came across the term. Willard goes into great detail in explaining Lectio Divina in his book, *Hearing God; Developing a Conversational Relationship with God*, and also includes exercises so one can not only understand what he's talking about but practice this valuable exercise as well. Simply put, Lectio Divina means "divine reading."

Lectio Divina is a Latin term for the practice of scriptural reading, meditation, and prayer intended to promote communion with God and to increase the knowledge of God's Word. Lectio Divina has four separate steps: read; meditate; pray; contemplate. First, a passage of Scripture is read, then its meaning is reflected upon. This is followed by prayer and contemplation on the Word of God.

In the first step, one is encouraged to read (*Lectio* = read) the Word. It's better to read slowly as to give the Word a chance to "sink in." I would advise that you don't start with a long passage but something fairly short as you develop your habit of using this method.

The second step is to meditate (*Meditatio* = meditate) on what you've just read. Stop, think, listen and let the verse marinate in your mind and in your spirit. Don't get in a hurry! Clear your mind, minimize distractions, relax, lean on the Holy Spirit for direction, insight, and illumination on the Word.

The third stage of Lectio Divina is prayer (*Oratio* = prayer). Here, in quietness and solitude, one communicates with the Father around the very scriptures you have just read and meditated on. Don't get in a hurry. Pray that the fullness of what you've read and meditated on becomes part of your being, and, that you begin to walk out these truths in everyday life. This would be separate from your normal everyday prayer in that it's specific to the truths you are reading and meditating on.

The fourth and final stage of Lectio Divina is contemplation (*Contemplatio* = rest). Here we let go of our own ideas and agenda. It is just simply, resting in the Word of God. You are now listening at the very deepest level to the Father Who loves to speak to us in that "still, small voice." Again, don't get in a hurry. You're in such a tender place with the Father that He can speak to you in a way that you are able to hear with incredible clarity.

These four stages of Lectio Divina are not at all intended to be legalistic requirements, and there should be no time frame or limit as to how long each stage should last but rather a proven way of reading, meditating, praying and then resting in scriptures that you have personally chosen. I would, however, suggest that you at least start by spending a minimum of 5 minutes in each of the four stages. You'll need to be disciplined to do this (which is another great habit). But, I believe that after a few times of putting Lectio Divina to use, and seeing the benefits, you'll devote more and more time to it in the future.

I fear that many won't give this method a chance due to the time investment involved. Our world is so fast paced, and we all have so many activities, most of which are very important, that we have a difficult time in devoting much time to things that are extremely important and that have eternal ramifications. Those who will commit themselves to it will definitely reap the rewards.

THE PROMISES OF GOD

"God has not given us hundreds of promises simply for us to read and enjoy. He has given them so we might boldly declare them to bring us victory, health, hope, and abundant life."

—Joel Osteen

There are many verses in the Bible that can be received as promises of God, or promises "from" God. Some suggest that the number of those promises might be well over 3,000! If you want to get the most out of your Bible reading time, start now keeping an eye out for some of them. Below are some of the more familiar promises.

But seek first the kingdom of God and His righteousness, and all these things shall be added to you.

Matt 6:33

Trust in the Lord with all your heart; and lean not on your own understanding; in all your ways acknowledge Him, and He will direct your paths.

Prov 3:5-6

Goodness and mercy shall follow me all the days of my life, and I will dwell in the house of the Lord forever.

Psalm 23:6

I can do all things through Christ, Who strengthens me.

Philippians 4:13

He Who is in you is greater than he who is in the world.

1 John 4:4

For the Lord has not given us a spirit of fear, but of power, love and a sound mind.

2 Tim 1:7

Those who wait on the Lord will renew their strength. They shall mount up with wings like eagles, they shall run and not be weary, they shall walk and not faint.

Isaiah 40:31

Train up a child in the way he should go, and when he is old, he won't depart from it.

Proverbs 22:6

Delight yourself also in the Lord, And He shall give you the desires of your heart.

Ps 37:4

And we know that all things work together for good to those who love God, to those who are the called according to His purpose.

Rom 8:28

And my God shall supply all your need according to His riches in glory by Christ Jesus.

Phil 4:19-20

Give, and it's given unto you: good measure, pressed down, shaken together and running over will be poured into your bosom. For with the same measure that you use, it will be measured back to you.

Luke 6:38

His divine power has given to us all things that pertain to life and godliness.

2 Peter 1:3

For whoever calls on the name of the Lord shall be saved.

Rom 10:13

Blessed is the man who endures temptation; for when he has been approved, he will receive the crown of life which the Lord has promised to those who love Him.

James 1:12

Blessed are the poor in spirit,
*   For theirs is the kingdom of heaven.*
Blessed are those who mourn,
*   For they shall be comforted.*
Blessed are the meek,
*   For they shall inherit the earth.*
Blessed are those who hunger and thirst for righteousness,
*   For they shall be filled.*
Blessed are the merciful,
*   For they shall obtain mercy.*
Blessed are the pure in heart,
*   For they shall see God.*
Blessed are the peacemakers,
*   For they shall be called sons of God.*
Blessed are those who are persecuted for righteousness' sake,
*   For theirs is the kingdom of heaven.*
Blessed are you when they revile and persecute you, and say all
*   kinds of evil against you falsely for My sake. Rejoice and be*
*   exceedingly glad, for great is your reward in heaven.*

Matt 5:3-12

And you will seek Me and find Me when you search for Me with all
your heart. I will be found by you, says the Lord.

Jeremiah 29:13-14

When you happen onto one of these promises in your Bible reading claim
them for yourself. Many of them are easy to memorize. Begin to declare them
over your life as the Holy Spirit brings them to your memory.

ENGAGE:

1) Look up these Bible verses and identify the promise(s) contained:

> Deuteronomy 31:8
> 2 Chronicles 7:14
> Jeremiah 29:11
> John 3:16
> John 8:36
> Philippians 4:19
> James 1:5
> James 4:7

2) How many promises can you find in Psalm 34?

3) Start a list of promises that are special to you.

Anytime I'm dealing with challenges in my life, which is nearly always, (LOL) I'll look in the Bible and find a promise that speaks specifically to the test that I'm going through. When thoughts of negativity come my way, I'll declare that promise vocally. It's amazing how the Holy Spirit immediately empowers the declaration! Try it!

EPILOGUE

By now, you've learned dozens of easy to understand principles, methods, tips, and techniques to help you with your Bible reading and study. I hope you've enjoyed the simplicity of these principles as I have found them to be extremely helpful to me in my journey with the Father. I also hope that you have picked up on the extremely practical nature of what I've written. You should now be ready to open your Bible and jump in with both feet with a new zeal, knowing that the Bible will begin to come alive like you've never seen it before! You should now be able to *Read Your Bible For All It's Worth!* Read, study, enjoy! A great adventure lies just ahead!

My prayer for you is that the respect, reverence, and love that I have for the written Word of God is imparted to you as you become a devoted student of the Bible—the Greatest Book Ever Written!

Thanks for investing your resource and time with what will be the first of many books to follow. I would love to hear your feedback on how *Reading Your Bible For All It's Worth* has influenced or helped you. You can contact me at:

ATRYB124@gmail.com

I would like to invite you to join my blog. I think you'll enjoy the wit, wisdom, and insight.

www.andytaylor.com

Join me on Twitter: @AndyrtaylorCom

I pastor Trinity Fellowship in Sayre, Oklahoma.

www.justasyouare.com

Services are on Facebook Live, Sunday Mornings @ 10:00 A.M. CST

ABOUT THE AUTHOR

Andy Taylor is the founder and leader of Trinity Fellowship in Sayre, Oklahoma. His ministry has been focused in helping people of all ages learn to relate to God as Father, as well as helping them find their individual gifts enabling them to be functional contributors to the Body of Christ. He's involved in giving apostolic oversight to a growing number of churches and ministries across the Western United States, Canada and Mexico. Andy's profound ability to make complex scriptural issues simple and practical is his key to "equipping the saints for the work of the ministry", and to have a living and powerful Kingdom church that impacts the community, the region, and the nations. A former professional bull rider, Andy was inducted into the Texas Rodeo Cowboy Hall of Fame in 2008. Andy and his wife Julie have been married for 42 years and are proud parents of five grown children and nine grandchildren.

Follow Andy on Twitter - @AndyrtaylorCom

Read his blog: "The Way I See It" - www.andyrtaylor.com

Trinity Fellowship, Sayre, OK - www.justasyouare.com

Email: ATRYB124@gmail.com